She Moves Mountains

A collection of real-life stories from women sharing the triumphs, trials, and tribulations of their professional journeys in career and entrepreneurship.

For permission requests, write to GCW Publishing House at:
team@thegreatcanadianwoman.ca
Published by GCW Publishing House and Media Group
www.gcwpublishing.com

Quantity sales. Special discounts are available on quantity purchases by corporations, associations, and others.
For details, contact the GCW Publishing House and Media Group head office at the address above.

Paperback ISBN 978-1-990370-00-7
eBook ISBN 978-1-990370-01-4

Edited by Christine Stock
Book Designed by Doris Chung
Cover Designed by Michelle Fairbanks
eBook by Ellie Silpa

Printed in North America

She Moves Mountains

A collection of real-life stories from women sharing the triumphs, trials, and tribulations of their professional journeys in career and entrepreneurship.

Amanda Lytle . Catherine Smith . Jane Middlehurst
Crystal Hardy Zongwe Binesikwe . Jessica Danford
Marsha Vanwynsberghe . Natasha Rueter
Stephanie Moram . Yulia Eskin

SARAH
SWAIN

Contents

Bios

Preface

Imagine if no one ever spoke a word about their journeys? The journeys that happen behind the scenes. Behind closed doors. Off social media. In our hearts. In our minds. In our souls. The journeys that keep us up at night. The journeys that distract us from everyday living because we can't wrap our heads around the paths ahead that we know are available to us. Imagine if no one ever shared the internal combustion we all feel when our decisions feel like the opposite of what the world around us expects us to make? Imagine a world in which we never shared our fears, our greatest acts of courage, or the moments we wanted to throw it all away and hide?

What a fictitious world that would be. What a dangerous world that would be, as it would normalize obedience without question, drive the depths of social conditioning, and adulate the idea of human perfection. This is the slippery slope we've been playing the game of life on, and unless more people share the figurative dirt and grit under their nails as they courageously carve their own paths, we leave more people behind us believing they don't have what it takes to choose and commit to the desired change they want to see in their lives.

At some point in our human history, we moved away from the wisdom of our intuition. We fell into the traps of shoulds, can'ts and won'ts in order to prioritize the peace and comfort of those around us. At some point we accepted living a societally or familial obedient life in exchange for our personal inner freedom. At some point we stopped trusting our innate and primal wisdom and started trusting experts, ideologists, educators, and other perceived authorities over our own inner knowing. At some point we put a greater value on accolades and achievements over joy and fulfillment. At some point it has become wildly difficult to trust ourselves to know our path and trust ourselves even deeper to carve it.

Yet even when faced with more mountains to climb than ever to just simply BE in our world, on our own terms, one thing has never fallen out of our scope. Our ability to choose. Everything we have, everything we do, and everything we want to have and do all begin with a choice to let ourselves have and do it. Our ability to choose ourselves is a superpower, granting us with the life of our dreams—if we let ourselves.

The SHE Series has been created from the realization that the more we normalize courageous journeys, the less courage our future generations will actually need in order to simply live on their terms, make the decisions they choose to make, and carve out the future they know they deserve. The women who share their stories in these books are blazing trails for generations to come, and I am deeply honoured we get to play a small part in the impact they're here to make.

Stay tuned at GCW Publishing House as the SHE Series grows and as we work together to normalize what it means to live life on our own terms.

Thank you for reading and for supporting our incredible authors.

In gratitude,

Sarah Swain

Founder, GCW Publishing House

Intro

It shouldn't be this complicated. We shouldn't have to ask ourselves if we're too old, if we belong, if we're capable, if we're skilled enough, if we're too late, if we're allowed, if [insert whatever other doubt exists in our minds as a result of what we have been conditioned to believe]. So, guess what? This unnecessary level of turbulence that enters our lives when we are simply making decisions to put us on a more fulfilling path gets to stop. It just gets to stop. The moment we recognize the difference between our personal path (our truth) and the path that has been constructed for us (social and familial conditioning), everything gets to change. It is our birthright to design a life we love, and the beauty of it is that our personal and professional journeys are unique to us. What we view as a successful professional life is decided by us. Our permission to forge a path forward isn't determined by paper, it's determined by our heart and determination.

How exciting is it to know that there isn't a single person on the planet in charge of your future other than yourself? Or perhaps the weight of that responsibility feels heavy, knowing it's all you and no one else? Which, by the way, is entirely understandable too. Ownership is both empowering and daunting. You know deeply that you're capable of creating a life you love, but the responsibility of it all feels like too much to take on. The conversations with people. The explanations for why you think and dream the way you do. The justification of your choices. The unsolicited opinions about why you should just play it safe and do something easier. The boundaries you need to erect and uphold in order to preserve your precious energy, and the inevitable loss of relationships as a result. The assumptions that you must not be grateful for what you have or appreciative of what you've been given. The consistent actions you need to take and decisions you need to make also seem to never end. Like dang, right?! It's no wonder people play small and stick to the beaten trails.

If we really think about why this struggle even needs to exist in the first place, it's because we have accepted the ways of our society, family, and culture as a way of being, and without question. We're born, and then through a series of conversations, examples, and teachings, we accept it. We absorb the beliefs of others and make them our own without even realizing it, then at some point in our lives, we crack. The *mid-life crisis* is a very real thing, only it can happen within a person at any age, usually when one comes to realize they have spent their time focusing on the things that didn't matter as much as they once believed, and they now fear they're running out of time to get it right. The sports cars, the designer handbags, and the expensive trips are simply a way of obtaining a temporary satisfaction that they're doing what they want to do, *dammit*, only for their reality to continue persisting the longer they try and resist it. Ah, *what you resist persists*—a philosophy of the late Swiss psychiatrist Carl Jung. And how true? So, what if we stopped resisting what feels right and true for us by finding the courage to make it so? What if we spent intentional time building our level of self-belief? What if we learned from a young age to discern between our true beliefs and why we hold them versus beliefs that have been instilled within us without our permission or knowing? What if we went against the grain and started doing things differently? Perhaps even backwards from what the proverbial assembly line of life has attempted to predetermine for us? Imagine!

This is why we share. To normalize self-trust. To normalize trying new things. To normalize living against the grain others shaped for us. The more we share, the more we flick the switch within others that they, too, can create their own future the way they want to experience it. By sharing, we remove stigmas. By sharing, we mitigate the fear of the unknown for future generations. By sharing, we reduce the unnecessary amount of friction we face even still today, to simply work the way we want to work.

Let the stories of the women in this book inspire you to make the choice to create a professional life on your terms, to commit to your decision, and to start taking the necessary actions to help propel you there.

Chapter One

Finding Home: An Immigrant's Search for Belonging

Yulia Eskin

Some could say that the life they lived is not at all the life they had imagined for themselves. Nonetheless, at only thirty-five years of age, I can say with certainty that absolutely no one could have predicted the life I'd have. I was born in the USSR, a country that no longer exists. My mom was rushed to the hospital with me on the night of the Chernobyl nuclear explosion,[1] and perhaps that was a sign for the grand change that was about to take place on that side of the world and in our lives.

I couldn't have imagined then that I'd immigrate three times, live in four countries, and end up in San Francisco, the world capital of innovation. Or that I'd eventually leave a high-paying and prestigious tech career to start my own leadership coaching business. I never thought that I'd live away from my *very* tight-knit Jewish family *and* marry a non-Jew (yikes, thinking of my parents' reaction to it would give me heart palpitations). Certainly, I couldn't have guessed that I wouldn't become the computer science professor that I wanted to be and would instead work for startups and enjoy it. And I most definitely had no idea that I, who never wanted to be a leader, would end up leading multimillion-dollar projects.

My personal success story is in many ways not my own. In my family we often talk about our immense fortune of being born at the exact right time in history when it became possible to leave the USSR[2] and find a home, first in Israel, then in Canada. My parents immigrated twice to provide me with opportunities to live a different and better life than they had. My cultural heritage of education and success also played a big role in my story. My father, a Jew in the USSR, was subject to a racial quota for Jews and was not given equal access to a university education. In more recent history, many in my family tree were murdered during WWII, both by the Nazis and their own fellow men.[3] It's hard to imagine a life of such marginalization, yet I admire the zest for life and resilience that I see in my parents despite all they've been through. This story of success is our story.

My Identity as an Immigrant

I've spent my entire life being a minority and the "other." A Jew to the Russians, a Russian to the Israelis, and an immigrant to the North Americans. And then, of course, a woman in tech, a highly male-dominated field.

I never thought much about my identity until my move to Canada. I was seventeen years old, and for the first time, I had to choose whether to identify as Russian or Israeli. In Israel, Russian Jews were not seen as "Jewish enough" since they were forced to give up Judaism in the USSR,[4] thus identifying as Jewish only culturally and ethnically. At the same time, I never appreciated how Israeli I was while living in Israel, although I'm genetically 99.8 percent Jewish. It was in Canada, when meeting non-Israeli Russians that I finally felt Israeli. It was culture, shared history, and upbringing that made me more Israeli than Russian. A shared language alone did not guarantee belonging with Russians, just as shared genetics by itself did not make me Israeli.

I felt happy to have a strong sense of belonging. Until somehow, and unbeknownst to myself, I became Canadian too. I remember a trip back to Israel when I sensed something different about myself. A discomfort. It didn't fit like a glove anymore. It felt different. *I* felt different. It was home but not home at the same time. I missed the multiculturalism of Canada and the tolerance, politeness, and openness. I started noticing the judgment of people around me, the normalized chauvinism and racism. I started feeling ashamed that I hadn't seen it before. In the beginning of my life in Canada, I couldn't understand what multiculturalism was, exactly. Was there a new culture created from many cultures or were there just many separate cultures with no common thread? What connected people if not their background? I

I only wanted to belong, in the simplest possible way.

didn't believe in it and thought it was merely something people said. But somehow, I began experiencing it myself and missing it in my old home country.

Unconsciously, I started searching for my identity. As much as I enjoyed the process of discovering new countries, people, and traditions, I felt somewhat betrayed when my own identity seemed to slip away from me. It felt like a stone that detached from a large rock that was now moving through unfamiliar places, never able to return. I was losing my grip on my identity, and I couldn't hold on to it anymore. I couldn't claim with conviction anymore that I was just Israeli or Russian.

The passage of time changed who I was, and what I believed in, without conscious effort on my part. And I hated the messiness of it. I wanted to . . . belong. In a clear way. I wanted to say, "I am . . ." and be done with it. I didn't want to embark on a long story of all of my immigrations every time I was asked where I'm from. I didn't want to discuss the politics of the Israeli-Palestinian conflict, just as I didn't want to be the activist for women in tech. I didn't want to become a symbol for my communities. I only wanted to belong, in the simplest possible way. I wanted to get all the cultural references and to know the traditions and children's songs. And animal baby names. I once left a baby shower crying because I only knew three out of twenty baby animal names. I just wanted to know them and not be reminded of my foreignness, again and again.

Sadly, the more I adopted my new culture, the less of a belonging I felt in my own immigrant communities. In North America, each immigrant chooses her own identity. On the spectrum of assimilation, many lived externally Canadian lives while holding on to their cultural values, resisting change, and being frustrated by those who questioned their beliefs. I remember a fiery debate with a group of Russians about gender roles, many feeling a career woman who chose to remain childless was an odd biological outlier. Some immigrants would completely reject their background and blend in. Even in an immigrant community, finding your own people was a bit of a challenge. It felt as if the number of people with whom I could truly belong was shrinking dramatically.

At times, comfortable in my North American identity, something would happen that would so sharply remind me of who I am. When anti-Semitic attacks happen, the fear comes back that the sense of safety that I usually feel is an illusion. On a trip to Spain five years ago, I visited Toledo, which once had one of the largest Jewish communities since Biblical times. When Spain unified into a country, Jews were forced to convert to Christianity. Alternatively, they could leave, or they could remain and get executed.[5] As I sat in a café eating albondigas across from a church that was once a synagogue, the tears started streaming down my cheeks. It's hard to explain the feeling of pain and loss I felt for what transpired there 500 years before. It's often easy for me to suspend my own Jewish identity as an atheist, but in such moments, it's as if I'm transported to a different era, sensing the betrayal these communities felt from their own neighbours and being reminded of the persecution and displacement my people faced and still face today.

Then the horrible guilt kicks in, for blending in and not doing more to preserve my cultural roots. Like clockwork, guilt shows up when I test the boundaries of my identity. Dating and marrying a non-Jew? Losing some fluency in my native tongue? Visiting a church with my husband's family? How far can I go before the guilt shows up to beat me into shape? In a nation that fought so often for its survival, I feel most guilty for having the ability to walk away from it and blend in.

I slowly started to realize that I will not fit like a glove in any of my cultural homes. Just as I have an accent in every language I speak, I "fit" everywhere with a slight "accent." Almost, but not quite. Was it time then to redefine what is home?

Identity and Career

In Hebrew, there's a saying, "Am Israel Chai," which means "The people of Israel are alive."[6] It's a bittersweet proclamation said with pride, celebrating survival and success against all odds while remembering a painful past. For Jews, the shared pain is a driving force for success. As a child of immigrants, I always felt the need to justify the great sacrifice of my parents' two immigrations. The necessity to make something of myself and to build a foundation in a new land for the next generation has always been tremendous. As is the internal pressure to live a worthy-enough life. Therefore, success, for me, became an act of defiance, belonging, and heroism.

After merely a year in Canada, I started my university education in computer science. I always loved math. Luckily, I wasn't raised with the familiar stigma in North America that math is hard or that it's not for girls. I began seeing the damaging effects of this type of thinking when I started doubting my own abilities as a woman in tech once exposed to such ideas. My classes had only a couple of women, but I felt too embarrassed about my accent to approach anyone. In those first few years, talking to people from other cultures was a challenge, and days would go by without me uttering a word. A female professor pushed me to attend a conference that would later become the largest in the world for women in tech. I remember walking the long hallways, and I couldn't believe my eyes. There were about a thousand of us, all girls, and so many dressed in a feminine way. At that point in my life, to fit in and not draw attention to myself, I was dressing down to appear less feminine. I was also trying to be overly rational and reject my intuition and emotions. But at that conference, I shockingly realized that I had developed a belief that as a feminine and emotional woman, I didn't belong in tech. A woman who belongs in tech has to look different, I thought, by wearing dark colours, no makeup, hair in a ponytail, and definitely no heels.

Discovering research as a career direction and the fascinating area of artificial intelligence was a major turning point for me. Until then, I hadn't really considered going to graduate school, but I was hooked by the idea of creating human-like intelligence. Fast-forward a few years and I was a master's student doing research. At first there was no doubt in my mind that I'd continue to a PhD and become a professor. My grandma liked to joke that once I'd become one, I'd be able to buy them an apartment where they'd live comfortably (they still live in subsidized housing in Israel). I loved to think of myself as an academic, and soon enough, I began to work as a researcher. For the first time, I felt that I was with my people. I loved the long intellectual debates and how smart, ambitious, and idealistic everyone was. I felt at home, at last.

Only that these were some of the hardest years of my life, as I started suffering from severe anxiety. I couldn't focus, I cried nearly every day, and it would take an immense amount of effort for me to get any work done. I started coming to the crushing realization that I didn't like research itself as a career. I panicked that I'd need to leave the home I found and start over. I felt like an outcast, knowing the negative perception of the tech industry in academia, and I didn't want to be judged for "stepping down." At the same time, I imagined the industry had a more utilitarian mindset and would see me as too idealistic, rigorous, and boring. I also surprised myself by realizing that I actually didn't enjoy working alone despite being an introvert. I wanted to be part of a team, building important technology that had a significant impact.

It was a blessing in disguise when my research got defunded, a common occurrence in academia. I was twenty-six years old, and I remembered an old dream of working in the world capital of tech: Silicon Valley. Leaving my family to embark on my own immigration was both a frightening and an exciting prospect. In our culture, girls often stay home until marriage, so moving out a few years earlier was already a huge deal. Knowing the challenges of immigration, it wasn't easy for my parents to let me go, but they did. They supported my dreams. I had one life to live, and for me, if I was going to work in tech, I only wanted to be at the top. Once that was my goal, I was determined to reach it.

Moving to San Francisco felt like being in a movie where all the apps on my mobile phone came to life as the physical buildings I'd regularly pass on the street. Airbnb, Google, Uber, Netflix . . . it was beyond exhilarating. Everyone was in tech, and almost everyone was a software engineer too. What I loved most about people was the passion. Most were on a mission to make a difference, to build the next big thing, and to make it big. As people often said, "To work hard and play hard." I started working at a startup as a junior software engineer. Despite having two degrees in computer science, I didn't have any software development experience. I saw on my co-workers faces that they had little confidence I'd make it there. But I wasn't going to give up and turn back. I worked non-stop for many years. I made mistakes but never the same one twice. I knew that what I didn't have in experience, I had in perseverance. One of the biggest lessons (and frustrations) in my career was that I always cared more than everyone else and that's why I spoke up, stood out, and eventually moved forward faster.

I made mistakes but never the same one twice. I knew that what I didn't have in experience, I had in perserverance.

Leadership

I never wanted to manage or lead and often shied away from such opportunities. The fear of failing, disappointing others, and my need to please people always stopped me in my tracks. Culturally, women weren't seen as leaders, so I imagined a life as an individual contributor until one day, a year into my first job, my manager declared that I have natural leadership skills and that I should become the technical leader on my team. Each of my peers had at least a decade of experience, and I was quite intimidated. No one had ever explained to me what leadership meant, and I was too scared to ask. I remember my shock, and the shock of my family, that I could be a leader. Not knowing much about my new role, I reluctantly jumped in. My habit of caring too much compensated for lack of experience, as it drove my curiosity and steadfastness. I soon started setting direction for my team, representing it to stakeholders and making technical decisions.

I finally realized why I was chosen for this role over others. I learned that leadership meant being proactive, communicative, and pragmatic while having an opinion. I saw that many of my colleagues were too set in their ways to compromise and struggled to articulate their work. My gift was that I was a big-picture thinker who could also dive into the details and communicate to audiences of different technical levels. I discovered that I had a passion for product development and empathy for the end user, while most engineers were only focused on the narrow scope of their work. As a leader, I was able to translate between product managers, user researchers, and engineers, all of whom had their own language. Ironically, I found myself as a chameleon, moving from one work culture to another, something so familiar to me as a child of immigrants.

Throughout my career, I fought with my femininity, cultural values, introversion, and imposter syndrome. I didn't see myself in others around me, and it played tricks with my mind. I sought closeness and genuine connection with my American male peers, while they didn't. I cared about the mission of my work and not just the technical details. I didn't go home to work on programming side projects, and it made me wonder whether it meant that I didn't belong in tech. I discovered other women felt it too. As a female leader, I was afraid to be seen negatively for being assertive while also fearing being soft would hurt my authority. As an introvert, I had to work hard to speak up in a room full of people, with guilt and second-guessing hitting me after every sentence. My people pleasing was agonizing, and with every step forward, I felt pulled back by insecurity.

Bit by bit, I got better at trusting myself and seeing the value I brought. Personal growth was so intimately linked to my growth as a leader. As Brené Brown said, "Who we are is how we lead."[7] I learned to be more patient with others as well as with myself. I saw that cultivating strong bonds and team trust helped in moments of crisis and deadlines. The "no blame" culture led to more collaboration and self-expression. One of my co-workers came out to me as gay. Another talked about his challenges with mental illness. I truly wanted people to show up as their full selves, and it began to happen for all of us. I was taken aback that being who I am and trusting myself was what my team needed. And what the tech industry needed too.

Leading became one of the most rewarding experiences of my life despite challenges of getting promoted in contrast to my male colleagues. There were times when I was being asked to do the work of a leader without the title and recognition. I used to think that leadership was reserved to a certain class of people that didn't include me, but I then discovered the importance of taking action *before* seeing myself as a leader. In fact, I became a leader rather than having been born one. We often can't imagine a certain path for ourselves simply because we're lacking role models who look like us. Our identity can also limit us in pursuing opportunities and dreaming new paths. As an introvert, I didn't know I'd enjoy a team environment and even leadership. I thought I couldn't work at a startup because I was risk-averse, but I then saw how much I enjoyed the curiosity and independence a startup allows. Looking back, I recognize the key is not to limit yourself based on who you are or who you *think* you are. As you grow in your career, you change as a person and with it, the next opportunity ahead.

Challenges in Tech and Transition

My thoughts about transitioning out of tech began with a traumatic bullying experience by a male co-worker, who in the tech industry, is referred to as a "brilliant jerk." He's typically a smart and highly product- ive engineer who creates a toxic work environment. Sadly, he often gets promoted the fastest since individual productivity is valued over team success. In contrast, many women, including me, build high-achieving teams by collaborating and mentoring. However, the values by which we operate often aren't represented in promotion rubrics.

One of the pivotal points in my career was when I was being bullied by one such engineer. Tech is abundant with challenging personalities, but in this case, I felt targeted. He was one of the early hires and became an essential go-to, although he didn't share his knowledge willingly. It got bad when he stole my work assignments and humiliated me in team meetings. He publicly denied me any help, which affected my ability to do the work. Management and HR ignored offence after offence, asking me to deal with it on my own. They even discouraged me from making an official complaint, saying they wouldn't protect me from retaliation. I was shocked they were protecting him instead of me.

It was one of the worst periods of my career. I never felt so helpless, anxious, and betrayed. I dreaded waking up and going to work. My confidence was plummeting, my focus started to deteriorate, and no one was stepping in to help. I also couldn't leave the company, as my ability to live in the US was tied to my employer. My hands were tied and all I could do was hope for the better. Then he was promoted and celebrated by the same managers who had witnessed the bullying I was going through. However, the cruellest consequence was doubting my place in tech. For twenty years since I started studying computer science in junior high, I never questioned whether it was for me . . . until that point. That's when I began wondering whether this was how the rest of my career in tech would be. Would I be fighting one jerk after another while not being promoted by inadequate managers? Was this stressful and demanding job worth it? For the first time in my life, I started considering leaving tech, and it was unbelievable to me that I was becoming part of a statistic.[8]

There was also a lack of role models in leadership in which I could see myself. Most of the male leaders had kids and stay-at-home wives, and I wondered how I would fare as a mom in tech. Sadly, there weren't many female leaders who I could identify with either. The more I grew as a leader, the more I wanted to invest in people rather than in technology. I felt an internal shift happen, as if my brain switched from left to right. Instead of fixing society's problems with technological solutions, I wanted to work from the inside, making society itself better and more humane. And hopefully, changing the tech industry in the process.

I was struggling with guilt over even considering leaving tech for several reasons. On every measure, I had a better and easier life than my parents could have had. I was working at a prestigious job and earning a big salary. I lived in the centre of innovation, and at least on paper, I had made it. It was my dream as a woman and an immigrant to get to this point, especially in my early thirties. It was unfair that my sister whose work changes lives was making a lot less. I was so fortunate and had so much privilege as a white and university-educated woman that wanting more and looking for my purpose seemed ungrateful.

There was also the guilt of abandoning the "movement" of women in tech. I met many older women who described much more challenging experiences in their careers yet persevered. They deserve all the credit for why it's easier now to be a woman in tech than it was before. I thought so many times about how much my grandma and mom could have achieved had they been born in Canada. How things would have been so much easier for them. It pains me that I have so much more privilege than they could ever dream of. And even that is not enough for me. I felt like I was chasing my tail, trying to punish myself for the success I had out of the pain for the opportunities my family didn't.

At the same time, I lost both my aunt and grandfather within a year. Their deaths were so sudden, and they shook me to my core. Until then, I hadn't experienced death as an adult and simply couldn't grasp that they were forever gone. It still brings me to tears that I won't again hear their voices calling me "Yulichka." Their deaths made me question everything. I valued well-spoken intellectuals who were high achievers, but it didn't occur to me how rich and beautiful my relatives' lives were, being full of meaning and family. I was in my early thirties, unmarried, and childless, and I had so many career aspirations. I looked down at the domestic and simple lifestyle. I was always afraid of dying young, so I raced to the top to achieve in case my time was cut short. Their deaths forced me to reexamine what truly mattered to me, and it was connecting to and affecting another's life in a meaningful way. Bonds and relationships. It was seeing myself back in Canada with my family, witnessing their daily life and growing old with them. I wanted to feel again part of a large multigenerational family that was so familiar to me from my upbringing, which was a stark contrast to my North American life of ambition, individualism, and isolation.

Over the next few years, I found myself discovering the coaching field. I was afraid to step into something so entirely different than tech. Would I still be a woman in tech if I'd become a coach, and would I find belonging in my new coaching community? I didn't see myself as an entrepreneur, but I wanted more freedom, flexibility, and the ability to make an impact on people's lives. My work in tech was important, but the impact I wanted to make now was different. I wanted to touch people's hearts and change their lives. I wanted to empower other immigrants like me to move beyond the point where they started in life and the limits in their mind. If anything, my life was showing me how far one can move from the circumstances they were born into. And once again, as with every other transition in life, a new identity was born.

Lessons

One of the biggest lessons in my life thus far is that people can reimagine themselves. Our identities are not static. Our starting point is only a variable not a prophecy, and often we can't even imagine what is possible. As a deep thinker, I was shocked to see that taking action significantly changes the person I become. It changes my identity over time, and it opens new paths that I could have never seen before. I started from wanting to understand and define my identity so that I'd have a place to belong to. However, since transitioning into coaching, I began to find a home within my own self. What was different this time? I was becoming aware of my values of freedom, connection, and curiosity. In the midst of the COVID-19 pandemic, I started one of my biggest adventures: I became an entrepreneur and a career coach. I'm early in this journey, but it's already the most peaceful and happy I've ever felt. Living in alignment with my values, experimenting, challenging myself, and making an impact on people's lives as a coach has been the home that I was searching for for so long. I sense that there's still a lot of change ahead, but this time I accept the unknown and don't limit my future based on who I am now.

Since becoming a coach, I've been questioning whether I'm no longer a woman in tech and whether my two-decade affair with it was a mistake. Part of me wants to hold on to the romantic idea that I have a single purpose, career, or identity and that life's mission is then about uncovering it. The truth is that these three things change with me. Every step I took in life was meaningful to me at the time, every decision was right for me then, and every challenge provided a way for me to reflect and grow as a human being. Each stage in life brings its own experiences, desires, and meaning to me. I finally feel more at peace that as I make decisions and take action, I change as a result, and with it, my aspirations, values, and direction in life.

We don't invalidate the past by growing, changing, and making new choices for ourselves. The pressure to find that elusive purpose, identity, and worth dissipates when I begin to trust that every step I take is the right one for me. I now realize that I don't have to choose between being Russian, Jewish, Israeli, Canadian, American, or between being a researcher, software engineer, leader, or a coach. I'm all of these things, and every single version of who I am had its place in my growth. I'm all of these, and they all inform my knowledge and worldview. I love being an immigrant for the many gifts it's given me in my life and career. I love being multicultural, understanding many languages, and connecting with people who are different from me. I know I've lived an unusual life, and if the past is any indication, I'm only excited for the unexpected that's in the future. Finally, as I reflect on who I was a decade ago and who I am now, I'm curious about who I will be in a decade, but I no longer try to find a box to fit in. I am simply myself on the big adventure of life. I'm worthy, and I am my own home.

To my parents, Inna and Dmitri, I dedicate this chapter to you. You are my two great loves. Thank you for being the dreamers you are and for having the courage to chart new paths for our family. Thank you for your sacrifice, for making me the dreamer that I am, and for supporting my endless adventures. To my sister, Anna, who knows me better than any soul on earth, I'm so grateful for the bond we have. To my husband, Mark, my best friend and biggest fan, I love your tender and gentle heart. You're the most precious gift life has given me. To my grandma, Luba, our matriarch, you are one of a kind. Thank you for teaching me strength and wisdom. To my aunt, Ella, who left us too early, thank you for your tenderness and love.

To the rest of my family, you're always in my heart.

Yulia Eskin is a first-generation immigrant from Belarus. She grew up in Israel and Canada and now lives in San Francisco with her husband, Mark. She is deeply passionate about the human experience and personal growth that immigration brings forth. She loves talking about culture,  technology, and leadership. She has longed to find belonging and has discovered the beauty of multiculturalism. Her dearest friend once told her that we all cry and laugh for the same reasons, something Yulia has never forgotten. She considers herself a global citizen.

Yulia has reinvented herself multiple times, from being a researcher in computer science to a software engineer and leader in Silicon Valley to her latest passion: career and leadership coaching. She has worked for health-tech companies, has led multimillion-dollar projects, and has been featured in *Business Insider*. Through her path, she has learned many lessons about communication, management, and empathy. She loves to coach engineers on their leadership skills so they can unlock their full potential and reach their dreams. She believes introverts, women, immigrants, and other minorities are indispensable in tech.

Yulia values curiosity, insight, and deep connection. She hosts workshops for engineers and created a conference to celebrate immigrant success stories. She discovered that entrepreneurship brought her peace and purpose once she started living in alignment with her values.

Chapter Two

Mic Drop

Stephanie Moram

The more we live our lives to the tune of our own drummer, the more authentic, peaceful, and powerful we are.

-Richard Bliss Brooke[1]

I dropped the microphone.

Palms sweating. Heart racing. Words disappearing from my mind. Standing on a stage in front of 500 people, I literally dropped the mic. Clinging to the pages of my presentation for dear life, all I could think was *Why am I even up here? Who wants to hear what I have to say? This is stupid. I should just turn around and leave—save myself from embarrassment.*

When I finally looked up from the paper being held by my trembling hands, my fears were confirmed—people. Lots of flipping people. So many people staring at me expectantly, waiting for something to come out of my mouth.

Come on, Stephanie, the voices in my head yelled. *Just say it. Say your first word. They are waiting for you. Say it. Say it!* I thought about bee-lining it to the left side of the stage. I even glanced over to see how far I would have to run. Standing alone on that stage was scary AF, and I am surprised I didn't vomit in that moment. But with the knowledge that I'd come there with a message I believed in, I finally began speaking, one word at a time.

"Be real. Be true. Be beautiful."

To my amazement, no one interrupted me. No one walked away. No one laughed at me. No one smirked. They just listened to me. They actually listened. And when I was done? They clapped, and I survived.

You see, I was never one for public speaking. Even as a child, I disliked reading aloud in front of others. I was the kid hiding at the back of the class, trying not to draw attention to myself while the teacher picked someone to read aloud. I'd always loved the words and the stories and the messages one could learn from what we were reading, and I have vivid recollections of listening attentively as my teacher read to our class. It was one of my favourite parts of the day, yet also one of the most terrifying. As each minute passed, the fear would set in deeper and deeper. I knew exactly what would come next.

"We are going to go around the class and each of you will read a sentence out loud," she'd say.

Next, she'd ask who wanted to go first. *Not me*, I yelled in my head. *There are zero ways I am going first. If I go first, I am more likely to be laughed at.* Therefore, I made no eye contact and pretended as if I didn't hear anything. *Maybe if I look away, she won't call on me first or at all.* I slid further and further into my chair, until my knees almost hit the ground.

(That was my MO. That would be my MO for a large part of my life.)

Back then, I developed a strategy to cope with my fear: I'd silently count how many kids were in front of me before it was my turn to read. Then I would count the sentences to find the one that would inevitably be mine to read. At eight years old, I understood that if I practised over and over in my head, I was less likely to make mistakes. It was the perfect plan, and I did this routine every single time we were asked to read aloud.

Despite my best efforts to disappear into the back of the class or to pronounce the words just right, my greatest insecurities were exacerbated when I was told I would be held back in grade three. All my friends moved onto grade four; it was a really difficult transition for me. I remember the exact moment I was told I was "redoing" the third grade. I begged my parents to not let that happen. I cried for days, maybe weeks. There I was, a fourth grader in grade three, convinced I was not good enough or smart enough.

Looking back, I wonder if anyone noticed my extreme way of coping with reading. Did my teachers catch on to how nervous I was to read out loud and just chose to ignore it to make me feel better? Were they completely unaware of my inner turmoil?

As an adult, I better understand the physical reactions I experienced at the thought of using my voice. While sitting in class, my leg would shake. I didn't pay much attention to it, but now I can see how anxious

I was. My body was essentially going into fight-or-flight mode. My heart was pumping out extra blood to my muscles, getting me ready to run. Run right out of that class. My breathing would speed up and my mind was on high alert; I was hyperaware of my surroundings and of all the terrible things that could happen if I tried to speak. I didn't want anyone to laugh at me if I did, in fact, mispronounce a word. *What if the other kids think I'm stupid? What will happen if I completely mess it up?*

These are the same anxious reactions I experienced nearly three decades later, standing in front of large audiences and knowing they were expecting me to enlighten them with an empowering and witty message.

I've always had a message to share, but actually getting it out there has not been my strong suit. Being afraid to speak in front of groups of people spiralled into the larger issue of me not feeling heard by friends and family. When I'd speak up, I was often interrupted, which left me feeling dismissed. When I brought an idea to the table, it was ignored more often than not. Without my ideas being validated, it felt easier to remain silent. Why speak your mind if no one listens to you?

My younger self was prone to meltdown after meltdown because I didn't have the emotional intelligence to express how I was really feeling, and I wasn't taught how to express myself in a positive manner, which pretty much instilled in me that speaking up doesn't work and no one cares what you have to say.

The fear of using my voice to create space for myself and my ideas continued throughout my adult life. I shied away from sharing my thoughts, from contributing to conversations where I could have added value, and most definitely from speaking in public. Whether I was a third grader in the back of the room or a successful entrepreneur, I cared too much about what people thought of me. I didn't want the negative attention; I didn't want to fumble my words. My fears crippled me. They perpetuated my belief that I didn't have anything meaningful to say or share with others. After years of being dismissed and ignored, I honestly didn't think anyone wanted to listen to me. The voices in my head had all but convinced me it wasn't even worth the effort.

There was a peace in my silence. I was able to grow a successful business, build meaningful relationships, and raise a family. I was doing everything "right." But here's the thing about stifling your voice . . . you still have beliefs, opinions, and ideas. And as I evolved and learned, I had some pretty remarkable, life-changing ideas—ideas that others could benefit from, if I was only willing to speak up and share them.

But speaking up is for other people. The kids who volunteered to read in class; the people who didn't drop the mic during their first speaking event, I thought. As comfortable as my quietness was, I knew that I needed to connect with a larger audience. As part of my business, I'd learned so much about how to make the world a better place, improve our communities, and live fuller lives. These were valuable insights that others would greatly benefit from. When I learned of a huge network marketing event, the voices in my head finally said something useful: *You should speak there.* Then the doubt, insecurity, and general overwhelm settled in. When I casually mentioned it to my mentor, he encouraged me. He believed my words had value. He believed what I had to say mattered. So, I took a risk to pursue something that I deeply wanted, I emailed the organizer of this massive event, and guess what?

Ping. You've got mail. "We would like to invite you to speak on our panel of rising star entrepreneurs in Las Vegas. Please let me know if this is something you are interested in." Plus some other words, but you get the idea.

Wait. What? I stared at that email in disbelief. I think I reread it ten times to make sure it was actually addressed to me and wasn't a mistake. It wasn't. I'd put myself out there, asked for exactly what I wanted, and here it was: my chance to speak up, my opportunity to prove that even if my voice shook, my message was more important than my fears.

For the first time in my life, speaking in front of people was a "heck yeah," and I might have squealed a little with excitement. Even still, as I began typing my acceptance response, the doubt crept in. *Everyone will laugh at me. Just you watch. This will be another time you fail. This will be another time no one will listen to you. So why bother? You have no clue how to speak in front of that many people. Seriously. Who do you think you are? There are so many more qualified women to speak. They probably made a mistake.* Before I had time to change my mind and convince myself that it was a bad idea, I squashed all that negativity and hit that send button, accepting the invitation to speak in front of 2,500 people.

Leading up to that day, I watched videos of other speakers at past events over and over to see what questions might be asked. It was my tried-and-true practice method from grade three. I thought preparation and planned answers would alleviate my anxieties. On the contrary, as I sat and skimmed through the videos, it brought back all the emotions I felt when I was asked to speak up in class.

Fortunately, I was no longer a fourth grader in grade three. I was a grown woman with a successful business, and I wanted to empower others. How could I do that if I hid away? A lightbulb went off. I realized I had been too busy focusing on what I didn't think I could do, what I could not control, and what people thought of me instead of what I was great at.

That was my turning point. My perspective on myself changed; someone believed in me enough to ask me to be on their stage. And this someone was incredibly smart and talented. They didn't just ask anyone to be a guest on their stage. I took a step back and accepted that I should be honoured. Heck, I was honoured. And dammit, I had something valuable to share.

Relinquishing my fears as best I could, I started focusing on all the good I had to offer and letting my true self shine. I had a message that needed to be heard. Instead of practising what I was going to read, I

Instead of practising what I was going to read, I needed to practice not being held back by other people's opinions.

needed to practice not being held back by other people's opinions.

Suddenly I could better appreciate my experiences growing up, as well as my "disaster" of a first presentation. Our traumatic experiences often shape us, but they don't have to define us or entrap us in incorrect beliefs about ourselves.

When I finally walked up on the stage in my black shirt, black jeans, and high heels, the voices in my head were good to me: *They will listen to you. They want to hear what you have to say. You have something important to say. They will smile. They will appreciate you. Go be a badass.* The butterflies stayed, but my self-talk calmed my nerves. I felt ready. When I'd looked out into the audience, there was a sea of faces staring at me. These were people who wanted to hear my opinions, people whose very presence validated my voice and my worthiness of being on that stage. I grabbed the mic firmly and proudly spoke up.

I remember the feeling of complete relief as I walked off the stage—I was so thankful I didn't trip. By doing what was actually right for me, by finally using my voice, my physical agitations dissipated. My shoulders had lowered; my tensions had subsided. I faintly remember someone saying, "Good job!" in the background.

I did it, I thought to myself. *Time to celebrate.* What was most surprising was the number of people that approached me to tell me how much my message resonated with them and how it had helped them see their own potential.

Some complimented me on how articulate I was, and others said I didn't seem nervous at all. It was crazy (and validating) because I'd thought I was talking too fast and looked like I was hit by a train of nerves. Apparently, I hid it well. After the positive feedback, I felt like I could confidently share my messaging again—if given the opportunity.

Sooner than expected, I was presented with my next opportunity. Once again, I felt my nerves creeping up, but this time it wasn't because I thought people weren't going to listen or because I had nothing important to say. I was nervous because I was going to be speaking on a large stage; this time I'd be speaking to 5,000 people. Insert gag reflex here.

Before my presentation, I paced back and forth in the hallway for hours, repeating my speech in my head. I received a few funny looks as people passed by and watched me talking to myself. And when I stepped onto the stage, I said exactly what I had gone there to say. Did I nail my presentation? Not really. But when I chose to use my voice, people clapped and said thank you. A few people even asked to take a picture with me. That caught me off guard, and I had to clarify they'd meant me: Stephanie Moram. They then graciously laughed and said yes.

Confidently speaking to that many people was freeing; it was evidence of how much I had grown in confidence. However, the evolution and up-levelling continues. Every time I step on a physical or virtual stage, I continue to grow, learn, and discover more about myself.

Accepting the fact that I do have something to say, and that there are people who want to listen and learn from me, took time. I didn't all of a sudden release all my self-doubt or nervousness. But instead of consistently putting myself down and being my own worst critic (because I was so good at doing that), I began to heal and allow myself to be heard. We are all worthy of being heard.

The conviction that comes from believing what you say—that was the game changer for me. Silencing the voices that perpetuated my insecurities and doubt started when I cared more about people hearing my message than I did staying safe.

I started sharing my knowledge with people as best I could. I did one live video after another. It was daunting at first, but it prepared me for those moments on the big stages. I put sticky notes on my computer to keep me on track while speaking. I practised over and over what I was going to say until I didn't have to stare at a paper all the time. I accepted constructive criticism from my mentors, as hard as it was at times. I learned not to care if I stumbled over my words while speaking, and to not take myself so seriously. When I accepted the fact that some people will laugh or be critical no matter how well I speak on a stage, I was free to share my truth and make the impact I so desired.

The more times I stepped on the stage, the easier it got. The more I trusted myself, the more natural it felt. I will never stop being nervous when invited to speak on a stage. My hands will still get clammy, my voice will crack a little, and I will still get a knot in my stomach. The biggest difference is I now believe in myself when I am up on the stage. I believe I have a story to share. I believe there are people that need to hear what I have to say.

Ironically, and somewhat unfortunately, I still felt unheard in my everyday life. I felt dismissed. It was as if to escape those feelings, I needed to be on a stage. I was living in a parallel universe.

One moment I was confident and crushing it on stage, the next moment I felt alone and like no one wanted to hear me. My journey toward reclaiming my voice is still a work in progress. I am working on changing the narrative around "no one listens to me" to "everyone respects what I have to say, even my friends and family." I speak up more in everyday settings and am vocal about how I need to protect my space.

My public speaking journey continues as well. Email after email after email piled up in my inbox from CTV Calgary, NBC live streaming, CBS Sacramento, ABC Alabama, and the list continues. I was invited to share my top seven tips on how to live a greener lifestyle. *Did I read those emails correctly? How did I get to this place?* I had never spoken on

TV and had zero ideas of what to expect, but I said yes anyway, because when an opportunity presents itself, you say yes and figure it out later, right?!

It was comical how many times I walked around my house to find the perfect natural light for my TV segments and tried on what felt like ten different shirts to make sure I didn't fade into the background. I made sure my video camera and mic were working numerous times because I had had a dream that they weren't able to see me or hear me. What a disaster that would have been! So, I triple-checked everything. As I'd taught myself to do with my stage presentations, I shook off my nerves and put on a big smile. I knew exactly what I had to say. It was second nature for me to talk about green living. *I got this*, I said to myself.

And I did. Some of the best feedback I've ever received followed one of my most recent interviews: "You're made for TV. Knowledgeable and entertaining. The producer loved the segment." That sentence has stuck with me. It validated all the effort and time I have put into my business and career. Who would have thought back when I was eight years old that I would be on stages with 5,000+ people watching and on TV with millions of people looking at me? I learned to speak up, even when I was afraid.

You will be faced with challenges in your life, whether that is stepping on a stage, embarking on a new professional path, or being presented with a major opportunity. You can either keep believing the bullshit stories you are telling yourself and that your experiences have pro-grammed you to believe, or you can jump and see what path will open up for you. You don't need to have all the answers. You don't have to continuously second-guess yourself and your abilities. You don't have to live a life without confidence. You don't have to live in fear. You have it within you to be whatever it is you want to be.

I never wanted to be a speaker; I never wanted to be the one on the stage. I was terrified I would embarrass myself or say something silly or look like I am about to do a somersault because of my constant jazz hands while talking. As a kid, I dreamt of being a lawyer and going to school for five million years. I couldn't really tell you why. Oh, wait. I watched so much *Law and Order* as a teenager I thought that was my path. Fast-forward to university, and law school was not on my radar. I went down the psychology trail and became a social worker for Child Protective Services. Not exactly the spotlight type of job. After two maternity leaves, I took a chance—a chance on myself—which led me to where I am now.

It's hard to imagine how different my path would have been had I allowed my mic drop experience to be the first and the last time I stepped on a stage; so many people wouldn't have heard my message.

I'm not sharing my story to impress you but to impress upon you that anything is truly possible. Your past doesn't define you, as clichéd as that sounds. It is absolutely true.

Never in my wildest of wildest dreams did I ever think I would be sharing stage after stage or be seen on TV with incredible, inspiring, and powerful humans making waves in the world.

When I said yes to that first opportunity to get up on stage, I didn't know what was to come of it. I stepped outside my comfort zone and into the light. As messy and scary as it was to speak in front of an audience, I found something I didn't know I was looking for: I found my voice. I found my purpose. I found me.

This is just the beginning, and I know there is so much more good coming. I am grateful for each person who has given me the opportunity to use my voice and for each person who has listened when I've spoken. I'm grateful for all the people who supported my crazy dreams, including the ONE I didn't even know I was dreaming.

All eyes on me and no dropped mics, right?! What a beautiful feeling.

To my amazing husband, JP, for supporting me on this wild and crazy ride. Thank you for believing in me and for all your unconditional love. I love you!

To my mentor and dear friend, Richard Bliss Brooke, who taught me how to use my voice and gently pushed me outside my comfort zone. Thank you for all your tough love when I needed it most.

Stephanie Moram is a Green Living Mentor and the CEO and Founder of Good Girl Gone Green, where she teaches busy women how to live greener and more sustainable lives without feeling overwhelmed.

Wanting to reduce the number of unnecessary and potentially harmful products she was bringing into her family's home, Stephanie began DIYing her own cleaning and personal care products. Now with more than ten years of experience, she has helped more than 20,000 women to not only live more sustainably but also to live with less, to shop ethically, and to reduce the overall amount of toxins they are exposed to.

With a combined social following of more than 45,000, Stephanie has spoken at events like The Most Powerful Women in Network Marketing, Slay Online Sales Summit, and Be True Brand You. For her expertise, she has been featured in the *Wall Street Journal*, CTV Calgary, NBC Live Streaming, ABC Alabama, CBS Rhode Island, CBS and ABC Sacramento, CBS Connecticut, *Huffington Post Canada*, *Vegetarian Times*, *Green Child Magazine*, BlogHer, and Care2.

Stephanie lives in Ste-Therese, Quebec, with her partner, JP, and two kids, Ella-Jade and Jackson.

Chapter Three

Spirit Adventurer: Reclamation of an Anishinaabe Storyteller

Crystal Hardy Zongwe Binesikwe

Write the wrongs.

In the bright light of a spring morning, I sat down at my orange 1970's vintage typewriter to write my death story. I hadn't slept in days. The dark circles that framed my eyes were mirrored in my coffee cup. It was weeks into an emotional flashback when I told myself, "I can't do this anymore," for the last time. The smooth beige keys clacked as tears swelled my eyes. Seeing my truth drying on the page made my Spirit sink.

Early this morning, Crystal Hardy, aka Zongwe Binesikwe, was found unresponsive. Despite their best efforts, first responders were unable to revive the 38-year-old Anishinaabe storyteller from Thunder Bay. Hardy had a history of complex PTSD, which triggered days of suicidal thoughts, ultimately resulting in her death. Sources close to Hardy said they thought she was doing fine because she never asked for help. In truth, Hardy openly spoke about her struggles with complex PTSD and regularly promoted mental health awareness. A service will be held later this week.

Living with complex post-traumatic stress disorder (PTSD) means dealing with feelings of abandonment, dissociation, and toxic shame, as well as having suicidal thoughts. For me, the emotional flashbacks are the worst. I am overwhelmed with the same intense feelings of fear, shame, and despair that I felt having lived through years of emotional, physical, and sexual childhood abuse.

Many Indigenous people with complex PTSD are misdiagnosed by their health care provider and mistreated by the health care system. As an Anishinaabe nurse practitioner working toward a PhD in nursing at Queen's University, I knew this information would be important to my research.

As I reflect on how my life has changed, it helps me see the sacred spiral of life and appreciate that life unfolds in cycles. I am so honoured to be able to share my journey of self-exploration of my true soul's calling with you.

In my Anishinaabe culture, we introduce ourselves with our names, clan, and community to help situate where we are within the world. In an effort to reclaim my culture, I use *Anishinaabemowin* in my introduction:

"Boozhoo! Crystal Hardy nindizhinikaaz. Zongwe Binesikwe nindizhinikaaz Anishnabowin.

Makwa nindoodem. Binjiitiwaabik Zaagiing Anishinaabek niin nindoonjibaa Thunder Bay, Ontario nindaa," which translates to "Hello! I am Crystal Hardy. My Spirit name is Sounding Thunderbird Woman. I am part of the Bear Clan. I am a member of Rocky Bay First Nation, and I live in Thunder Bay, Ontario."

My journey into my true life's purpose started when I was gifted my Spirit name, Zongwe Binesikwe. In my culture, our Spirit names help guide our life's purpose. Before colonization, our Spirit names would also guide the community members in helping develop those strengths. These gifts would be supported and encouraged by the community as a whole. You would, in essence, be your Spirit—the embodiment of true soul's purpose.

I was also gifted the name Spirit Adventurer. One of my healers was excited to hear of my experiences and said that I have an adventurer's spirit. This is the journey I continue to embrace in an effort to reclaim the parts of me that were lost through colonization.

Colonialism can be understood as a set of ideals that involves unequal power relations between two territories, which creates "the other" or "the colonized." Colonization in Canada includes the attempted assimilation of Indigenous people into Western culture through the residential school system, sixties scoop, and child welfare system. There have been many devastating effects of colonization on the health of Indigenous people in Canada. If you are interested in learning more about the history of colonization in Canada and recommendations for reconciliation, I encourage you to read The Truth and Reconciliation Commission of Canada's Calls to Action.

Decolonization, to me, means reclaiming what has been lost or taken and honouring the gifts we still have. Decolonization is making space for Indigenous and other ways of knowing alongside Western ways of knowing. In an effort to decolonize myself, I started to attend powwows.

Powwows are traditional gatherings meant for individual and community healing and celebration. Seeing the dancers in their ceremonial regalia made me yearn even more to reconnect with my culture. Hearing the beat of the drum reconnected me with the heartbeat of Mother Earth, which led me to participating in a women's drum group and birthing two hand drums. Learning traditional Anishinaabe songs helped connect me to something greater than myself—to my ancestors, to my Spirit guides, and to Creator.

Through my own healing, I started remembering the teachings of my ancestors. I remembered that I am a sacred part of creation. I remembered that life has so many gifts to experience. I remembered that I am one of the *Oshkimaadiziig*, New People, of the Seventh Fire Prophecy of the Anishinaabe. The Seventh Fire Prophecy states that *Oshkimaadiziig* will find elders who have fallen asleep and wake them up to share their knowledge, leading us all to the Eighth Fire Prophecy of an eternal Fire of peace, love, brotherhood, and sisterhood.

As I attended more powwows, I felt nudged to go in the circle and felt an overwhelming urge to dance. I could feel the healing energy and the sacredness of the space I was in. Over time I learned to jingle-dress dance. The jingle dress, or prayer dress, is made from multicoloured fabric decorated with metal cones, or jingles. As the dancer uses light footwork close to the ground, the metal cones jingle sound to bring healing to those who are sick. I am so honoured to receive this beautiful gift. This connection to Spirit changed my outlook on life. In an effort to make sense of my life purpose, I decided that I needed to know my Spirit name.

Traditionally, in my culture, you would receive your Spirit name at a young age. Due to colonization, many of our teachings and ceremonies have been nearly forgotten. During my naming ceremony, the Elder burned tobacco as an offering to Creator while offering prayers to the Great Spirits of the Four Directions.

We sat in the darkness with only the sound of the Elder's song and the beat of the drum. I could feel my ancestors around me. The joy was growing inside of me as I felt the drum. When the drumming was over, the lights turned back on. The Elder spoke and gave me my name, Zongwe Binesikwe, Sounding Thunderbird Woman.

At the time I had no idea how to say my name, or how I would ever use it in my life. The Elder explained that part of my journey was to understand what Sounding Thunderbird Woman means to me.

Thunderbirds are large bird-like *Manitous* (Spirits) that travel through the clouds during storms, creating thunder with their wings and lightning from their eyes. They live in all four directions and carry messages from Spirit. They are the most powerful beings and can turn into human form by pulling back their heads like a mask and taking their feathers off like a cloak.

The power of the thunderbird was within me, which was terrifyingly awesome. My connection to Spirit was growing stronger each day. However, the more connected I was to Spirit, the more disconnected I felt to my material possessions. This disconnection was at odds with the life I had already created for myself. From high school on, I had been a high achiever, determined to break the cycle of disadvantage in my family. I graduated a year early from high school with advanced standing. I graduated from a three-year compressed program for my bachelor's of science in nursing with first-class standing.

After working as a registered nurse in an acute care pediatric unit, I returned to my studies to pursue a master's in public health with a nursing specialization. During that time, I also obtained my nurse practitioner certification. A nurse practitioner is a registered nurse with advanced training and knowledge, with many overlapping skills as a family physician. In my role as a nurse practitioner, I was able to provide primary health care in many Indigenous and non-Indigenous communities. During this important work, my eyes were opened to the systemic racism facing Indigenous people within the health care system.

My Spirit felt pulled to find ways to create positive change while bridging both Western and Indigenous worlds. Creator presented a new position to work as the regional Indigenous representative for a cancer care network in my region. In this position, I was able to advocate for the primary health care needs of Indigenous people at academic conferences, in newspaper articles, and radio interviews. I was so fortunate to meet many amazing people, including another regional representative who was a huge inspiration to me.

I remember seeing her stand up in the room and speak about colonization and the need for change. Although she was met with much resistance, she did not falter. She addressed each comment respectively, even when she did not receive the same in return. She was different than anyone I had seen. I wanted to know her and learn how to be so confident. I had to learn how I could be a more effective change agent in promoting social justice. So, I prayed.

I asked Creator to help guide me. The message I received was beautiful. I was told that if I do something for the greater, I am always protected. I was reminded to embrace my Spirit name—Sounding Thunderbird Woman. I was being called to use my voice and raise thunder in conversations to create change. By sharing my healing journey, I could inspire others to do the same, while combating stereotypes and promoting unity. I could use my privilege to access platforms that could educate the public about the realities of intergenerational trauma and the importance of sharing Indigenous ways of knowing. I was also being called to share my voice in different ways.

I created a podcast called *Under the Same Stars* to promote decolonization and reconciliation by highlighting people creating unity in their communities across Turtle Island, or North America. I share my personal narratives of my healing journey reclaiming my identity as Zongwe Binesikwe. *Under the Same Stars* has given me the opportunity to witness and share the stories of many brilliant people.

In an effort to explore other avenues to share my voice, I volunteered as a programmer at our local community radio station. I was inspired by Gord Downie's *Secret Path* album of the life and death story of a young Anishinaabe boy, Chanie Wenjack. Through this album, many Canadians started becoming aware of the legacy of residential schools in Canada. I saw the power of how music could mobilize fans into social action and created *Zee's Place*. On *Zee's Place*, I "decolonize your airwaves" through music and storytelling, featuring Indigenous and non-Indigenous artists promoting social justice and reconciliation. Music is decolonizing and healing, not only in songs of protest but through the self-expression of the artist and the emotion evoked in the listener, which aligns with the oral traditions of storytelling in my Anishinaabe culture.

Bridging Anishinaabe and Western ways of knowing can be a tricky but beautiful dance. Working in a colonized environment while embracing my spirituality has led me down the path of success over fulfillment.

With all the opportunities presented to me, I started to stray from my self-care practices. I got caught up in the competition and ego-driven world of journalism. I was overwhelmed with how horrible people were treating each other and felt unable to make any foreseeable changes. With all the lateral violence in my environments, I didn't realize how I was self-sabotaging as the darkness crept back in.

I texted my best friend those three little words I promised to never speak to anyone. "I need help."

"I can't do this anymore" was only a whisper as I carefully typed out goodbye letters to loved ones. I even wrote my own obituary. My only solace was the quiet ding at the end of each line. As my emotions rose, the keys were harder to control. My fingers furiously smashed at the typewriter until I collapsed.

With my body heaving on the floor, I struggled to find my phone through my tears. I texted my best friend those three little words I promised to never speak to anyone.

"I need help."

And before I could change my mind, she was there at my side, ready to help me in any way she could. Creator reminded me that I have supportive and loving people in my life. I remembered how much I needed ceremony and self-compassion.

Having complex PTSD means that I struggle daily with thoughts of self-loathing and disdain. My inner critic is so harsh and loud that it convinces me that no one wants to hear a word I'm saying, that my story doesn't matter and that I should kill myself to save everyone, including myself, the pain of my existence.

There are days I feel that no matter how smart or dumb I appear, kind or tough, pretty or ugly, hardworking or playful, it will never be good enough for anyone else. And in a lot of ways, that is the truth. If true, so what?

I need to be fulfilled inside of myself, not from anyone or anything else. This fulfillment takes radical self-love, care, and acceptance—something that most of us have not been shown before.

Embracing my true authentic self has been difficult but liberating. There have been so many pieces of me that I have given away or have been taken from me over my short time on this earth. And some days, I only see through anger and pain.

It's on those days I lean harder into ceremony and my faith in Creator. It has only been through ceremony and connecting to the land that has been healing for me. In fact, a few days after my friend saved me from ending my life, Creator answered my prayers again.

Once more, I spoke the words, "I need help."

But this time to my PhD thesis committee. For months I had been requesting to have an elder on my committee, not only as a means of decolonization, but for my healing and support. We had several meetings before this day that the Elder was unable to attend.

At the start of the meeting, I was disappointed to hear that the Elder may not make it again. But I was so broken that I told them I was suicidal. Moments later, the Elder joined our video call.

As I shared, the group held space for me to grieve. The Elder offered a ceremony to call my spirit back into my body. When our bodies experience traumas, we believe our spirits can leave our bodies entirely or in pieces.

The Elder could see only a small strand of my spirit still connected to my body. He grabbed this drum and started to sing. I let myself be healed by the drum's beat and his song, my tears nearly drowning me as I gasped for breath between my sobs.

The drum beat louder. Louder than my cries. Louder than my doubts. Louder than my fears.

I could feel my spirit returning to me. Pink returned to my face as the breath of life filled my lungs once again. My tears transformed to ones of joy as I felt the light within me.

The next morning, I returned to my daily ceremonial self-care practices. Creator was calling me to embrace my Spirit name, Sounding

Thunderbird Woman. Where was I being asked to make thunder? Where did I need to be a messenger? How was I already doing this?

The word that kept showing up was "storyteller."

Storytelling in my culture is essential for healing, teaching, and building community. Stories help guide us through the dark times and give us hope for the future. Children learn through stories, play, and song. As we share stories, we also share perspectives and understanding.

My storytelling includes journaling, writing, painting, and podcasting. Giving myself a "label" in this way affirmed how I felt inside. Using my voice as medicine has helped me work through unhealthy dynamics in my relationships, especially with myself, by forgiving those people who have hurt me. I am working on forgiving myself for the times I've hurt others and myself in my woundedness.

As I write the wrongs, I am able to heal. I ask Spirit to guide which stories want to be written, even when they are painful ones . . .

Sleep

Tonight he sleeps.
Which means . . .
So do I.

RE Memory

I can remember everything about that day . . .
I can remember everything.

Can I remember everything?

I can't remember anything.

I can't remember.
I can't . . .

I won't.

Secrets

I should have lied . . .
Said that everything's fine.

Kept quiet.
Kept safe.

Stayed in line.
Known my place.

I should have lied . . .
Should have said that I'm fine.

Stepped

        down

           and

       stepped

  Back.

I should have lied . . .
But I can't keep your secrets anymore.

As the words flow, the grip of grief lessens, and the anger subsides. My journal, a testimony to the darkest days, helps me understand that we are all stories. Our lives are merely chapters, and we are characters in our own stories. But not all stories are dark . . .

Blue Girl

Blue girl.
Yeah, you girl.
Boohoo, girl.
You're fine, girl.
You shine, girl.
All the time, girl.

Don't forget that.
We love you, my girl.

Portal

Sacred Womxn,

You are strong.

You are sacred.

You are passion.

You are womxn.

You are light.

You are ecstasy.

You are love.

You are sensitive.

You are delicate.

You are the sun.

You are the moon.

Sacred Womxn, you don't have to hide.

Or keep the scars inside.

You are sacred.

You are beautiful.

You are a portal.

You are adored!

Mama: Hello, baby.

Small One: Hi, Mama!

Mama: Can I tell you a beautiful secret?

Small One: Yes!

Mama: You are adored.

Small One: I'm not a DOOR! I'm a kid!

Mama: No, baby, "adored"—it means deeply loved and respected.
           You are so important to this world, to me, our Ancestors and
           Creator.

Small One: . . . Oh . . . I know!

The next adventure my Spirit wants to take is a deeper journey into my own stories—my cultural stories, my family stories, and more of my personal story. As I reconnect with my voice, I invite you to do the same. Your voice is unique, and your story is important to this world!

You get to write the next chapter in your life!

Chi miigwetch, Creator for this perfectly imperfect life.

Miigwetch to all of those who have come before me, my ancestors and relations.

Miigwetch to all of those who share space with me now, my children, my family, my friends, my supporters and loved ones, Sarah Swain, and the Great Canadian Woman platform.

Miigwetch to all of those who will come after me. Aho!

Crystal Hardy Zongwe Binesikwe (they/she) is a Two-Spirit Anishinaabe storyteller from the Bear Clan. They are a member of Biinjitiwabik Zaaging Anishnabek living in Thunder Bay, Ontario. For more information, please visit welcometozeesplace.com.

Chapter Four

TRUST

Natasha Rueter

It was an unfamiliar sensation, feelings of confusion, lack of motivation, and doubt. I started thinking, *Who am I? Who have I become?* I didn't recognize myself. It didn't feel good, and I had no idea how I let it happen. I told myself that it was my hormones, being pregnant with my fourth child. Part of me knew that wasn't the whole story, but now I have allowed myself to see the truth.

For as long as I can remember, I knew that I wanted to travel the world, marry someone I considered to be my best friend, have a house full of kids, own rental properties, and become an entrepreneur. It was my natural state of being to dream big, take risks, and follow my heart. I was happy, young, and carefree. I was determined, and no one was going to tell me that something wasn't possible. I started working at twelve years old. I bought a car at sixteen and moved eight hours away from home to finish my last year of high school without even having a place to live until I arrived. I didn't move because I needed to but because I was eager to absorb the world around me and everything in it. I became fascinated with people watching and was ever curious about the way people lived. I was never exposed to an alternative way of thinking or living at a young age, so over time, I started to think that something was wrong with me, as I didn't fit into what was considered "the norm." *Why couldn't I relate to others?* I didn't feel like I fit in anywhere, although from the outside, it may have seemed like I did. I struggled to connect with people on a deeper level, and I longed for genuine personal connections. I sensed a cloud of pain, fear, and negativity around everyone, but I wasn't able to put a name to all of this until now. *Why?! What did this all mean?* Thus, began my quest for truth and understanding.

That empty and bored feeling eventually became filled with the love and trust I have for myself and my desire to continue living life to its fullest.

As an introvert, I spent a lot of my time quietly observing people, trying to understand and find my place in this world. I felt alone in my bubble and too young to understand. I did not feel fulfilled with my education, or the many relationships that I had. Although it appeared to others as though my life was great, nothing resonated with me. I was living as I was "supposed to," but I felt empty and bored. I felt like there was so much more to life than we were led to believe, but I didn't have the tools to find it within. I can see now how money, power, and status have such a strong hold on our society and how they paralyze people from living their truth. This realization brought me so much freedom and joy. That empty and bored feeling eventually became filled with the love and trust I have for myself and my desire to continue living life to its fullest.

My personal bubble continued to ricochet negativity away from me. I never accepted difficult times or emotions as my destiny, just bumps in the road and opportunities to learn. Moving away from the victim mentality of asking, *Why does this always happen to me?* to taking charge of your life shifts your thoughts to *Okay, what opportunities will come of this?* I was always striving to find a better way. I didn't want to ever get comfortable with the status quo or to become stagnant. My strong will pushed through and said, *What do I need to do to be a better version of myself?* It wasn't until I found my soulmate that I felt that someone truly saw ME for me. I was still figuring out who I was myself, but I sensed a strong connection that I had never felt before. We are two very different people, but his openness and willingness to experience life was so refreshing. He wasn't afraid to be himself, nor was he bending to fit into societal norms. This connection was such a comforting feeling and the beginning of a wonderful adventure.

We soon found ourselves travelling the world from our home base in

South Korea. Having completed a university degree, and not jumping into a corporate job at twenty-one years old, was an easy decision for me. There was a deep knowing that I didn't want to spend my life in an office, becoming burnt out, unhealthy, and/or depressed. I had no idea what was possible at that time, but I knew there had to be a better life path for me, and I was determined to find it. It didn't faze me knowing that others didn't understand my approach to life, but I was grateful when my soulmate jumped into my bubble. I had so much trust in what was to come that there was no room for fear to penetrate. Now, whenever I plan a new adventure, I ask myself, *What's the worst that can happen?* My answer is never so bad, nor does it ever come to fruition.

At some point near the end of our time in Korea, I started to realize that what I had envisioned when I was younger had started to come true. I wasn't aware of the power of a consistent, clear vision until then. It was such a powerful moment for me when I realized I had, in fact, married a man I considered to be my best friend, travelled the world, bought a rental property, and started a family (yes, we had our first baby in Korea), and all by the age of twenty-six. As a teenager, I wondered how I would ever be able to accomplish that; it seemed so far-fetched and expensive, but I only ever let those self-limiting beliefs sneak in momentarily. The interesting part is that I wasn't pushing to make things fit, it just all fell into place, and not because I was lucky (I've heard that many times) or had money. NO, not at all. It was because I was very CLEAR about what I wanted, and didn't want, out of life, and I took ACTION toward the things that "felt right" for me. I was told many times that I was stubborn or didn't like to listen to anyone, but it was because I was the only one who knew what was best for me. Sure, things didn't always work out great, but I needed that experience in order to learn the lesson for myself. It's funny now that I have some strong boys of my own who are showing similar traits. Becoming a mother is a whole other can of worms. Every time I find myself wanting to tell them that something isn't a good idea, I force myself to pull back and choose my words and battles carefully. There will be times that they need some gentle guidance, and kind words of wisdom, but most of the time they just need to learn from their own experiences.

After having our first son, we felt the pull to come back to Canada to be closer to our families and have more children. We had purchased a house in Ottawa during our time away, so we had a house to come home to, but we had no way of making money. It wasn't easy for others to understand. *What are you going to do now? How are you going to raise a family without jobs?* I didn't want fear to dictate our next steps, and I didn't want to fall into a lifestyle that would diminish who I was just because I had a family now. If I would have worried about all the things that could go wrong, I wouldn't have experienced all the things that went right. My biggest takeaway from our travels was that happiness, freedom, and health are more important to me than status and a "secure job." (If that's what your goals are, great! It's just not for me.) I continued on in my usual stubborn and determined way, refusing to have anyone else raise my children and wanting to work for myself; so, I set out to start an in-home daycare. It was my first taste of business, and I loved it! I supported my husband while he studied to become a holistic nutritionist and personal trainer. Then my next exciting project began. I started my husband's fitness and nutrition business out of our basement. Brainstorming ideas, researching the best strategies, budgeting, marketing, and pulling it all together was so rewarding for me. It didn't even feel like work at times. These two businesses came together so easily because we truly believed we could make a difference in people's lives. Life was good; we loved working from home and being together in our own bubble. But then came my first life-slap in the face. My first taste of *I can't do everything that I want to anymore.* Having kids took a toll on me. I became resentful of their needing so much of my time when all I wanted to do was grow our businesses and buy rental properties. I had so much drive to DO and grow, but now life was yelling at me to slow down, just BE, and enjoy the kids. But I didn't listen; I hired someone to run the daycare, I bought two rental properties, and I became a real estate agent. Business was great, but I felt like I wasn't the mother I wanted to be or thought I should be (an unconscious self-limiting belief I struggled with for some time). I was pregnant with my third boy and at a point where I didn't want to spend another second playing Lego or singing the ABCs. I didn't want toddlers, I wanted grown children with whom I could have a conversation. I was screaming inside. *Why do I feel guilty for wanting to spend more time working than being present to my children's needs?* I continued to struggle with being present with my children for a long time. I'm not going to lie, I still struggle with it sometimes, but I have come a long way. The shift from being a multi-tasker to time blocking was a life saver. I struggled with the notion of families living in such an isolated environment while raising a family. The idea that everyone is out for themselves, don't ask for help, or talk about how they are feeling didn't make sense to me. It amazes me how alone one can feel in such a large city. After four years in Ottawa, I started to listen to that voice in my head telling me to slow down and be present. *Find your community.* We felt that our time was complete in Ottawa, and we began our quest for a slower, more intentional lifestyle on Manitoulin Island.

Moving to my hometown was an easy decision for us because it felt right and served as the next stepping stone for us. Others didn't see it that way. They probably thought we were crazy to leave our successful businesses behind and start from scratch in a small northern Ontario town. I've always had the belief that if you aren't growing or learning anymore, then it's time to move on to the next challenge or, alternatively, make adjustments to the current situation. Change is where I thrive! I had no idea what was next for us, but I knew business, health, and wellness would always be my passion. Again, I trusted it would all work out, and I stood strong in my bubble. Something good was on the horizon for us, I could feel it.

As we settled into our new community, I quickly realized a gap in the market and our personal need for accessible good quality food in the area. Two months after I delivered my third baby boy, I decided that I was going to open a health food store and café downtown. It was in my head now; it was going to happen. And so, my next adventure began. There were definitely moments when I thought, *How am I going to afford this? How am I going to pull this off?* And, of course, the naysayers chimed in: *A health food store doesn't work here. People have tried it already and failed.* Failure, like fear, was a word that just wasn't in my vocabulary. I looked at it as a challenge and a new learning opportunity. I knew that I had what it took to create a great store, and I just kept persevering. I trusted that it would all work out; we would be okay. Somehow, we survived with my husband doing multiple part-time jobs, me home-schooling my children, and all while creating a kick-ass business plan to attract the funding I required to launch my business. You really have to be willing to take on some risk to make the impossible happen. This business was a much bigger undertaking than I had taken on previously, and it was much more expensive. I understand the inner workings of financing and strategic planning, so it was no more than a fun puzzle for me. After getting approved for four different funding sources, I was on my way to opening my first store! A health food store and café in a small town. *What a rush, I did it! How did I pull that off?* The store was a bigger hit than I had ever expected. We knew our target customers well, and we created a culture around our shared passion for health, wellness, and local, organic foods. I have to admit, I had no idea what I was doing. I did understand a lot about business and finance, but more importantly, I stayed true to myself. If I would have overanalyzed every aspect before I opened, it would have never happened. I always prefer to "wing it" and figure things out as I go. This was an exciting time for me; we found our community of like-minded people and our little bubble grew. But being in the spotlight as an introvert was really starting to take a toll on me. I was not prepared for what was to come next.

Although my bubble was growing, it was also getting weaker. Over time I noticed that I was letting other people's negativities get the best of me. For so long I had held strong in my beliefs, but at a low point in my life, I let my bubble burst. I let other people's opinions and judgments in, and I got burned out. It got so bad that I had to sell my business. *Was it just my pregnancy hormones, or did I completely lose trust in myself?* It was a feeling I had never felt before. I started to take on other people's beliefs; I was even getting negative and judgmental myself. I found myself having a hard time being around people who didn't believe in what I believed in, and I started to lose myself, no longer recognizing who I was anymore. I started to believe that I shouldn't be running a business while I had four young boys to care for. Comments started to make themselves comfortable in my mind: *You shouldn't run a business like this or that. You only got the funding because of the way you look. Why are you moving houses again?* I started to question myself and my decisions. *Should I have a steady, safe job, with a pension and benefits? Should I stop going on international adventures while the kids are young? What is happening?!* I started to feel so lost and confused. I found myself reacting more aggressively. I said things that I wouldn't normally say, and as a result, I damaged some relationships. I felt that I had no choice but to sell. I gave up and started my deep dive within.

I isolated myself with a new baby, while my husband went back to school to become a massage therapist. It was another huge risk. It was a three-year program out of town, which restricted how often he could come home. With four children at home and neither of us working, it was going to be challenging. I knew it was the right decision and timing for him, but I didn't know who I was anymore. I was confused, and I could no longer identify what brought me joy or lit my soul on fire. So many business ideas came and went, and every time I would get close to launching something, I would feel this push to stop. I kept hearing myself say, *It's just not the right time. Keep going within, your time will come.* It was hard for me to DO nothing, even though I didn't feel quite myself yet. I wanted to work on a project. When I regained some of my energy after having my last baby, I accepted a "secure" nine-to-five job. It definitely wasn't what I expected, but this opportunity presented itself so easily, so I knew there had to be a reason. I enjoyed my work, I learned new aspects of business, and I learned what I needed to do better next time to become a better leader. I also gained a deeper understanding of the world outside of my bubble. My time there had a purpose, but it wasn't where I was meant to stay. During my last six months there, every cell in my body was screaming at me to get out. But I still doubted myself; I hadn't fully regained trust in myself. I started to believe for a while that this job was what I should do: *I have a family to support. I guess I need to suck it up*—an adage many people subscribe to. *Why am I now accepting this social norm?* It felt so wrong, but I still didn't listen to myself. This period of time was the longest I had ever let these limiting beliefs live in my conscious mind. I could feel my health slipping away in just that short amount of time. I had lost all clarity of what I wanted out of life and business. I never felt like a failure, but I sure was disappointed in the person I had become.

I look back now and realize how much I needed that dark time in my life. I felt the strong pull forcing me to go within to heal. This process helped me gain a deeper understanding and compassion for others and myself. Instead of judgments, I could see past people's behaviours and cruel words and feel their pain behind their actions. I understand that others' options are only a reflection of themselves. I have come out of this even stronger and more determined than before. The confusion started to dissipate once I realized that I had already accomplished all my goals; I needed to regroup and start again. At times I felt like I didn't have a purpose, and without goals, I felt lost. I started to brainstorm, but this time was a little different. Instead of focusing my goals on specific things that I wanted, I shifted them to how I wanted to FEEL (80 to 90 percent of the time). No matter what I'm doing

I am again committed to becoming the best version of myself with more love and intention than ever before.

in life, *I want to feel love and light. I want to feel present and grateful. I want to feel joyful and adventurous. I want to inspire, motivate, and share my knowledge. I want to feel strong and free.* Although I focused more on how I wanted to feel, I still set career and personal goals for myself. I wanted BALANCE. I wanted to run a business behind the scenes from home, giving me time to travel and move more freely. I wanted family time, personal time, work, and outdoor adventure, and to not feel limited in time or money. I am again committed to becoming the best version of myself with more love and intention than ever before.

As I wrote this chapter, I landed the job I had been envisioning (and yes, it's a job, not a business). I now get to work for a kick-ass online entrepreneur. I get to do what I love with so much opportunity to learn and grow in business and finance. I have the freedom to make my own schedule while working from home, and I don't feel the same pressure to have to work 24/7. Now that my husband has completed school, we made another huge life decision. We are moving across the country to British Columbia! Moving there has been a shared dream of ours since we met, and it's now in the works.

I started studying for my Master of Business Administration (MBA). I have learned that it's time for me to step way outside of my comfort zone in order to grow further, and not because of the MBA content, but because this school requires a lot of participation in class, online forum discussions, and a lot of group work. I could have easily taken the "safer route" and registered for the self-study program that has no peer interaction. Of all the decisions I've made in my life, this was by far the hardest for me. Over time, I acknowledged more of my own self-limiting beliefs, and I was determined to eliminate them. *I'm a poor communicator. I can't write. What do I have to offer to others?* Writing this chapter and speaking in front of a large group of people were things I never thought I could do before. Freeing myself of these limiting beliefs feels so much lighter, and I feel so grateful that I am able to share my story with you. I am still a woman of few words, but this is my way of paying it forward in hopes of inspiring even just one person to trust in themselves and to be free of unwelcome expectations. Much love.

Natasha Rueter is a tough woman. She has to be, having four boys and her loving husband filling her country house with noise, adventure, mess, and love. She has been in love with business her entire life and has always been captured by health and wellness. All of this came together with several of her business endeavours. She not only created a holistic in-home daycare while running her husband's personal training business, but she even gave the business away to an expecting young mother that she had employed. After buying rental properties and having been a real estate agent in Ottawa, it was time for her to change things up. Aside from loving business, travel, family, and health, Natasha adores and thrives on change.

Moving to a small town, back to where she grew up on beautiful Manitoulin Island, Ontario, Natasha set up a new business opportunity for herself. Reading the local market, she discovered a much-needed and missing piece; she opened her own health food store and café. It was, again, her own endeavour, and she wanted everyone involved to win. Her prices were fair, her authenticity was noticeable, and the store was not only a place to buy fresh prepared food or groceries but also became a staple within the area, creating its own community and subculture.

Now, Natasha is challenging herself to grow again by taking her master's degree in business, setting up her husband's new massage therapy business, participating at the gym, and doing yoga, hiking, camping, and travelling. Her favourite destinations are hot or rich with history but moving progressively forward.

Natasha is passionate, hardworking, patient, and loving, and she always tries to be the best version of herself. She lives without regrets and loves to look to the future possibilities that await her.

Chapter Five

I Had to Go First

Marsha Vanwynsberghe

I was the Queen of dabbling. In fact, I dabbled for years.

Being an entrepreneur wasn't new for me, it was in my blood. My first business was as a first aid/CPR instructor, and it was literally how I covered many expenses while in university. I started a personal training/post-rehabilitation business in 1998 in the small town of Tillsonburg, Ontario, where no one had even heard of personal training. For seven years, I was a co-owner in a brick-and-mortar training business. I have seen entrepreneurship from many sides, including this entirely virtual space that we are now living in.

Throughout the last twenty-seven-plus years, I worked as a kinesiologist. I was an entrepreneur working hour by hour and falling into physical and adrenal burnout a minimum of twice a year. Every single year it was a rinse-and-repeat process. I knew I was here to do more, to create something different or make a bigger impact in the world, and it took a family crisis, multiple breakdowns, and a pandemic for me to see how to make it a reality.

This story really starts in 2012 when our seemingly normal family began to experience substance abuse with our two preteen boys. It entered our home and never left. It grew as a monster that eventually took over all aspects of our lives. As a mother, I felt that I had failed everything and everyone, and it took me many experiences to realize differently. Through so many hurdles, broken-down moments, and lots of counselling and support, I found myself in a space of understanding that their journey was their journey, and I had to let go. This realization was not a one-step process. It truly took so many falls for me to look at my situation, our situation, differently. I had to find a way to take care of myself, to be a springboard for them if they ever decided to come back to us. I had to stop blaming them for their choices and take full ownership for my own. My health had fallen apart, I couldn't sleep for more than one hour at a time, and my nervous system jumped at the sound of a doorbell, all because I was living in a world that I never imagined I would sign up for. It was a gong show, and no words can ever do it justice. At the point of almost losing both of our boys only four days apart, both situations in our own home, I came to realize that I had no choice but to let go. If I didn't, I have no doubt we would all go down with the ship.

During this time, I started to understand the words ownership, choices, blame, radical responsibility, and the toughest one . . . surrender. From 2015 to 2017, I learned how to implement these lessons, boundaries, and self-care, and to let go of everything else. It's ironic when I now look back at that time in my life. The lessons in boundaries, ownership, and self-care would be lessons I would use for the years ahead. When I reflect on it now, I could never manage entrepreneurship without these pivotal pieces. Our business will only ever grow to the extent that we grow and care for ourselves. As an entrepreneur, we are our business on every single level. I have learned over the years that when I am feeling stuck in my business, it is because I am stuck in my personal life, and it always comes down to boundaries, ownership, and self-care. I swear my future self knew that I would need lots of practice in these areas.

In late 2016, a mentor asked me if I felt like we had made it through the hardest part of our journey, and I honestly felt like we had. She nudged me and said, "You know that you are obligated to show others how to do it too." That stung, yet deep down I knew she was right and that was one of the main reasons our family was given this chaos. I kept feeling called to write a book. In fact, I had felt called my entire life to become a published author. It took going through the worst experience of my life to see what my book was meant to be about. Over the next year, I dove deep into writing, and my first book, *When She Stopped Asking Why*, was released on November 17, 2017, on Amazon. This vulnerable deep dive into my story as a parent who finds her way when her life falls apart became a six-time Amazon Bestseller and all the private parts of my life became public knowledge. I had to grow into the person who could bring this story to life and was it ever a messy journey. Let me explain further.

My entire life I have been told things like "You're the strong one" and "You can handle anything" and "God never gives you more than you can handle." Family and friends constantly reminded me that I was the one to handle the "hard things." I repeated these words to myself when I felt like I couldn't do it any longer, but I can see now that these words made me push on, do it alone, and never show anyone that I was struggling. It became a badge of honour to be able to handle it all. I blocked others out, I didn't let them see I was hurting, and I rarely, if ever, asked for help. I got to the point that I didn't even know how to ask. When I felt like I would break down, cry, or throw in the towel, I would tell myself to keep pushing forward, but this pattern kept me on the loop of adrenal burnout that I mentioned in the beginning. This pattern also kept me feeling alone and literally alone because I couldn't and wouldn't let anyone else in. It all had to change because my survival depended on it. On top of it all, I was constantly triggered by people saying, "It's so easy for you because you are such a strong person." I didn't feel strong, I felt like I was failing everywhere.

Nothing about my journey or my story was easy, and the only way I could shift it was to start sharing my actual story with others. I had to let people see the real side of me, not the curated, hard-ass, strong-as-a-bull side. I started practising vulnerability, sharing my pain by sharing my emotions, and not living in or reliving the pain. I learned how to share the story and how it made and impact and affected me. I learned how to share the lessons from my story from my perspective while still being respectful to other people in it. By sharing my emotions, I was learning how to let other people truly see me, something that allowed incredible people to come into my life and build lifelong relationships with me.

Vulnerability saved my life, yet it was never easy. I fought hard to become me. It required equal amounts of working hard, letting go, and trusting the journey I was on. It literally all became a choice, because I couldn't go on living the way I was. It's a choice that any of us can make at any time. I recognize it's never easy to make this choice, yet it's never easy to stay stuck in a scenario that is suffocating the life out of us. I've said it many times, "We always get to choose our hard." I honestly am so grateful for these lessons because they have spilled into entrepreneurship and supported me more times than I can count.

I followed the nudge and started my podcast, *Own Your Choices, Own Your Life* in 2017. I knew I wanted to continue to normalize the process of people sharing their stories, especially their shame stories, to serve, support, and make an impact on others. I wanted to interview people and show others that we didn't have to give shame the power that we were constantly giving it in our lives. Deep down I can look at this progression and understand that I was learning how to share my own story by normalizing our shame stories. I was uncovering my actual purpose in this life. I wanted to help others and stop the endless suffering over our

To this day I still believe that our business will only grow to the extent that we grow ourselves.

stories. Ironically, I still didn't see it as a business, and I think that was a blessing in disguise. I spent this time learning about myself, my story, and shining a light on my purpose before I put that energy into a business. To this day I still believe that our businesses will only grow to the extent that we grow ourselves. I needed these years to understand the impact and potential reach of my message.

We always go first.

Throughout 2018 and to the end of 2019, I knew I was being pulled in a different direction. It wasn't just about me sharing my story, it was about teaching others to do the same. After many speaking engagements, podcast interviews, and coaching clients one on one, I began seeing the pattern that was unfolding. Women wanted to learn HOW to share their story, how not to be identified by it, and how to use their lessons to make an impact on others. I continued to stay open because

I believed I was being supported, and it would all make sense as long as I kept moving forward. The "problem" was that I was still working my full-time job, dabbling in my business in my spare time, and repeating the burnout cycle every few months. I loved what I was doing with my clients and podcast, but I simply couldn't figure out how to do it all. How could I leave my job when I wasn't making enough in my side business to make ends meet? In fact, I was barely making enough in my full-time job to survive, so how could I even think of leaving one stable thing to start something else? It just didn't make sense. People told me to just "burn the boats," and I would laugh and say, "You just don't understand." Our family had been hit financially for years with job loss and serious health issues, and we were scraping by with little income or money. So, I kept doing the only thing I knew how to do: work harder. I worked my day job, starting at the break of dawn training clients back to back all day, five days a week. I then ran from these appointments to the gym to maintain five to six workouts a week, then rushed home to try to learn how to build a business with whatever was left in the tank. Exhausting, right?!

In 2019 an internal shift happened. First, my husband lost his job, and I started to work even more hours in both jobs, which is absolutely not a badge of honour. I worked fifty-two weeks in 2019 and grossed $36,000 in my full-time job. I was beyond miserable inside. My body was screaming at me to stop, and I didn't have a clue how to do it. I was bringing in the only income we had, and I only had so many hours in a day, and it was never enough. I started to journal consistently and adopted the practice of script writing. Every single day, I wrote down statements as if they had already happened. For example, I wrote every morning, "I am so happy and grateful to retire from my training job by the end of 2019." I had no idea how I would retire, and I purposely didn't let my brain get sucked into the *how*. I just believed it would happen.

Christmas 2019 arrived and another burnout happened. The cycle was so predictable. By this time, I was crying as I pulled into the parking lot at work because I didn't want to go in. There wasn't anything wrong with my job, my co-workers, or my clients, I was just being called to something more. At the start of 2020, with no job change in place, I felt that I had failed myself again because I was in a new year and was still stuck in the same story. I broke down, I cried, and the anxiety of going back to my place of work became too great. I thought maybe if I changed locations, it would help. It's a tough spot to be in when there isn't anything wrong with your clients, your job, or the people with whom you work. The problem was that deep down I was being tugged in two different directions: I was living completely out of alignment and barely making enough to survive while busting my butt to help others with their health and lives. I was so done with all of it, yet I still couldn't see how to change it. I was betting on and giving to everyone else, but not myself. Yes, that was the missing piece.

I had to go first.

In January 2020, I moved to a different facility. This change created an opportunity to bring home more income, and I thought that an increased income would help me finally make the shift to working for myself in my coaching business on a full-time basis. Working out of a new location was exciting, but within a few days, I realized that it was not the only answer I was seeking.

My start date had been February 21, 2020, and on March 17, my governing college of kinesiology shut down my ability to work because of the COVID-19 pandemic. I remember the day so vividly. I went home after receiving the email and watched the world around me shut down. From professional sports to closed borders, global panic and lines at the grocery stores, I knew something life altering was happening in our world. I sat in deep thought that day, wondering what my next steps would be. As the world said it would pause for fourteen days to flatten the curve, my gut instinct said something else, and I had an honest conversation with myself.

"What if this is exactly what you wrote about in all of 2019? What if this is the opportunity you knew was coming and you have been preparing for?" And the kicker question, "Will I regret it if I don't choose to make the most of this time even if it is only for a few weeks?"

I woke up on March 18 and journaled, then decided that I wouldn't

It was time to learn from others and get to work.

allow myself to have any regrets about this "time off."

I didn't know what I didn't know. I had no idea where the clients would come from, who they would be, what I would offer, and how I would make it work financially. What I did know is that I had asked for time to work on my business, and this is what the universe was giving me. What if a global pandemic was the gift of time for me, and it was my choice as to what I did with that time? I knew the latter was the truth, and I wanted to live this time with no regrets. I wanted to see what I could create and who I could help. I kept hearing my inner voice say, "What if this is exactly what you asked for?"

I immediately jumped into service. When the world is in chaos and full of the unknown, people look to others for certainty and comfort. There were so many unpredictable variables at that time. I started offering Zoom calls, support, and coaching to help others know where to start. It's important to note that I actually didn't have the answers, none of us did, but I knew deep down that everyone would remember how we chose to show up during that time, so I decided to show up even if it was messy as hell. Messy action became my motto. Some days it was really messy, and when the doubts crept in, I reminded myself to show up anyway. I have proven over and over to myself before that I can find or create the answers when I get into action. Sitting, thinking, overthinking, and hoping are not solutions when creating a business. A business requires action and the ability to fall down, learn, rinse and repeat, and I did so much of that in 2020. My days were long, and when I wasn't helping others, I was committed to learning as much as I could about creating my business full time. I was ALL in, and the vision of my "safety boats" was getting blurrier and further away. I was losing my safety net and gaining my confidence at the same time.

I have always been inspired and motivated by businesses, female entrepreneurs, and success stories. So many others were creating six-figure and multiple-six-figure businesses, so I knew it was possible. I had proof all around me. I had no time for comparison or resentment. It was time to learn from others and get to work. I knew what I had to generate on a monthly basis, so I was focused on the numbers, yet I was open to seeing how many ways I could create it. I learned to be unattached to the how or the outcome, and I stayed connected to my faith that I would make it a reality. The classic zigzag picture of what entrepreneurship looks like, the roller coaster going up and down and all over the place . . . that was my life in 2020. People around me were complaining non-stop about the pandemic, what was right, what wasn't right, and they kept asking what I was watching on Netflix. I had no time for any of that. My self-care game amplified, I took care of my needs, I put my boundaries in place, and I put all my energy into faith and the belief that this business was happening for me.

I dove into my own personal story and recalled how I came to realize the need for radical responsibility in my own life and how it became the catalyst in my own growth and progression. I learned these lessons firsthand during our years of battling the chaos with our kids. If these lessons saved me then, why not focus on them again in this new stage of my entrepreneurial journey? I knew I could create something that would be valuable for others; we all have the opportunity to do so. I truly believe that we have everything we need to handle our circumstances, which is why we face our situations. Bringing on coaches and mentors help us amplify and speed up our progress, but we truly do have the solutions and answers within ourselves.

I focused on my strengths and my skill set and created a program to help women learn how to own their stories and use the lessons from those stories to build platform businesses to serve, support, and make an impact on others. I took the lessons learned from my story and built a coaching, speaking, writing, and podcasting business, so I am proof that it is possible, and now I teach others how to find their voice to share their message in the form of coaching, speaking, writing, or podcasting. My first group started in March 2020 and became a special "pandemic group." We learned together, we took messy action, and we embraced the roller coaster of a learning curve. I used every single bit of space in my new day-to-day life to learn how to grow my business, fine-tune my message, and pour back into myself. For the first time in my thirty years of working and serving others, I was able to start my days pouring into myself first. There was no more rushing out the door for a 6:00 a.m. client, and no more running through my day to only get back to my needs when my tank was nearing empty. Learning how to take care of my needs first became one of the biggest blessings of 2020. I listened to what I needed, what brought me joy, what didn't, what I wanted to do every day, and who I wanted to spend my time and energy on, and it allowed me to become a more finely tuned human, something that spilled over into my business. Slowly, it started to grow, and I was getting closer to meeting my previous income from my job yet in significantly less time than my typical forty hours a week. Don't get me wrong. I busted my butt, but I had energy left over. My husband noticed that I was happier and that I was creating something that mattered—something that had an impact on others. That was more fuel to keep going.

Here is how our habits, behaviours, and choices can own us if we aren't careful and conscious of what is working and not working. We all have a default system. All of us. We subconsciously go back to our default, no matter how much we have proven to ourselves over the years that it doesn't work. Unfortunately, that is exactly what I started to do. I started slipping back into my old default behaviours of working hard, pushing myself, building a business and income, and fighting to prove that I could make it work. No one asked me to prove that I could do it all; it was all me, and that is where ownership, boundaries, and self-care had to come into practice yet again. I actually didn't want to prove that I could build a business. I wanted to build the business and not lose myself to burnout in the process. That was the win I actually wanted to create. Yet during the early months of 2020, I was experiencing some unique symptoms such as toe numbness, hip pain, and back discomfort. I was not new to back pain. After more than ten abdominal surgeries and a full hysterectomy at a young age, pain was simply part of my life. I didn't give it too much thought. I saw my doctor, asked the questions, and waited for appointments after repeated cancellations due to the pandemic. If I am being honest, deep down I had a feeling that something was going on, yet I had no idea it would be as big of a deal as it turned out to be.

During the early months of the pandemic, I exercised from home, as exercise has been a huge part of my mental health support system over the years. I began noticing that some movements were getting harder to do. The symptoms persisted, and I was struggling to move at times, even when just walking. I remember being out for a walk once in the spring and having to stop because I didn't feel like my leg could continue. I felt like I would easily fall, and the pain only intensified. I figured I was sitting longer at my desk and that was the problem. My doctor requested an urgent MRI, as it was during the pandemic, no one was being seen and appointments were being pushed back. By late July, I knew deep down something was wrong. I couldn't walk for more than a hundred feet, standing was unbearable, sitting was impossible, and sleeping for longer than sixty minutes didn't happen. Fear was creeping in as I continued to work to grow a business out of thin air during a pandemic. Very few people knew I was struggling, and I trusted my instincts to not share it. I needed every ounce of time and energy for myself at this time.

In early August, after two cancellations, I finally had my MRI on a Friday morning. By Saturday morning, our local ER called, asking me to come into the hospital ASAP. I spent the next few hours listening to the doctors tell me that it was very serious, that I shouldn't have waited so long to be seen, and that I needed to see a surgeon immediately. It was a lot to process and take in. I sat there in the bed by myself, crying and trying to understand what was happening. The doctors repeated the MRI the next day, and within days, I saw an orthopaedic trauma surgeon. He informed me that surgery was my only option, and without it, I would likely lose my ability to walk. My L5 vertebrae had moved anteriorly by 1.5 centimetres, which simply meant it was damaging my L5 nerve. Now his next line was the kicker: Because of the pandemic, my surgery may be delayed for six to twelve months, and that was with me being at the top of the list. It was all so much to absorb while still trying to grow my own business. I was searching inside myself, trying to process everything, and I settled on the word "surrender." What if life was happening for me at this time? What if this was exactly how it was all meant to unfold? What could I control and what did I have to let go of?

Throughout August and September, I cried many tears and leaned into and on others. I couldn't do everything alone. By late September, I was scared. I couldn't walk, stand, or sleep. My past training clients were reaching out, wondering if we were going to get back to working together. I knew that wasn't part of my story, but I also didn't want to share it with others yet. As a known "queen of vulnerability" and believer in sharing stories, people didn't understand how I didn't share my news openly with others. Vulnerability is not verbal vomiting our lives to everyone, and vulnerability without boundaries is manipulative and has the completely wrong intentions. Vulnerability is sharing our stories with the people who have earned the right to hear them, and I needed every single ounce of energy for myself at this time in my life. It was time for me to be "selfish."

On October 1, my surgeon's office called. They had an opening on October 7, and I had thirty minutes to decide if I wanted to fill it. With a potential backlog of up to one year, I knew I had to take it. I had no idea how I was going to work, cover our expenses, and still build a business, yet I believed that life was teaching me some very valuable lessons. I embraced trust and let go of control. On October 7, I had an almost five-hour back surgery and spent the next five days recovering in the hospital. There were so many scary moments and surgery complications over those days, including two anaphylactic allergic reactions. I also lost a lot of blood and nearly received a transfusion, and my sodium levels plummeted below the point where most people don't recover. Add these things to being surrounded by people engulfed in fear, nurses working incredibly hard, and a global pandemic, and I know that I only made it through these days because of all the internal work I had done on myself over the past decade. All the mindset work and years of physical rehabilitation experience were meant to help me rehabilitate myself. My husband was unable to visit which made the days even longer and harder, so I leaned in. I FaceTimed friends from my bed, and I read my script I had written for myself for the hospital. I worked too hard to go out this way. This was not how my story was going to end.

Following my surgery, my surgeon informed me that the surgery had been a success but was far more complicated than they originally expected. I was full of titanium, with two rods, six screws, and a titanium cube. Additionally, I had a bone graft and fifteen stitches in my spine. The anaphylactic reaction to the surgical tape was worse than the surgery itself. I will always have scars where the tape burned into my skin.

The simplest things were the hardest. Getting in and out of bed, up and down from a toilet, and climbing stairs all required relearning. Getting dressed and putting on socks and pants was impossible. My recovery required more patience, compassion, and grace toward myself than ever. I am convinced that this experience happened for me to teach me that I had to learn to value and listen to what I needed. The days of pushing, burnout, and beating myself into the ground had to go. That first month was a blur as I learned how to move in my house and my life again. As the swelling decreased and I gained mobility, I could feel the difference in my leg. The nerve pain was definitely decreasing, and I was grateful for the ability to have this complicated surgery done. My family doctor later informed me that she had been scared as she watched my blood results come in while I was in the hospital. She said that some patients don't survive with the results I had. I knew it was true, and I knew I was here for a reason. I would not take it lightly.

Transitioning into home/work life post-surgery, still in a pandemic, and approaching yet another lockdown was no joke. I sat in deep trust as I was getting ready for the next round of my signature program to start in November. How could I possibly launch another round, do the typical launch strategies, and take care of myself? I didn't know how, yet I knew what I was supposed to do.

I purposely didn't follow up on old leads, and I didn't chase anyone down. I believed the right people would be there because of all the work I did in the past and all the value I had given to others. I would find my own ways to show up, be vulnerable, and share my message. As a result of this belief, I added five new women into my program who had reached out to me to get started. We launched our next round in November, and I created a monthly mastermind program to help women collaborate and build their businesses in this time of everything being virtual. As I finished 2020 and looked through my numbers with my accountant, I realized that I had created more money in 2020 through coaching than I did in 2019 with my full-time job. I was creating my own proof that I could do what fulfilled me, all while recovering from back surgery during a pandemic. I was validating my thoughts and wishes that if I stayed in alignment, it could be easy. I could create more income for my family while having more balance, joy, and free time. Now, don't get me wrong, I worked very hard. My efforts and time were intentional, and I learned to listen to and honour whatever my body needed. These were my lessons of 2020, and I am forever grateful for all of it. In fact, all the lessons in boundaries, self-care, and ownership continue to be pivotal in my personal life and business. I am my business, and how I choose to care for myself will dictate how my business grows. It always starts with me, and it always starts with you. We always go first.

As I start 2021, I am continuing to learn what works, what does not, and how to listen to what feels good or is in alignment with my vision for my business and life. After only a few months into 2021, I know that I am on track to create my first six-figure year in business. I made the promise to myself that I would replace my husband's income and that of my former job, and that promise didn't come from a space of ego or pushing. It came from a deep knowing that I am truly stepping into something beautiful and creating a life of impact. And that is exactly where I am supposed to be. The year 2020 happened for me. I needed the world to stop to see what I was capable of doing and creating. I had to stop the noise and instead learn to listen to what I needed. I embraced the space, the discomfort, and the lessons, and I know that is why 2021 is unfolding the way it is. It's a sign of all the beautiful things to come. My life is always happening for me, and by embracing my story and the lessons I've learned, I have found my strength and intuition. I will continue to pay that forward to show women what is possible in their own lives. I was not broken by 2020, although technically, I did break my back. The year 2020 made me, and I couldn't be more grateful for all of it.

I dedicate this chapter to my wonderful husband, Brad, and to all the amazing girlfriends, family members, and mentors who supported me through this process. I am grateful for the friends who were there for me unconditionally, and that I learned how to ask for help and allow them in. I learned to value myself, appreciate my worthiness, and receive the support of others. I honour everyone who was a part of my story because they have all played a role in who I am today. I am also thankful for my intuition and faith for guiding me through. I am here today because of them. I also want to thank my boys for being my best teachers. They have taught me how to love, accept, forgive, and truly live in gratitude for the moments that I used to take for granted.

Marsha Vanwynsberghe is the six-time bestselling author of *When She Stopped Asking Why*. She shares her lessons as a parent who dealt with teen substance abuse far past the level of normal experimentation. Marsha recently published a collaborative book called *Owning Your Choices*, sharing inspiring stories of courage from women around the world.

Through her programs, coaching, and podcast, Marsha teaches the power of Radical Responsibility and Owning Your Choices in your own life. She empowers women to own their stories, be conscious leaders, and build platform businesses to make an impact on, serve, and support others.

Chapter Six

The Safe Haven: Impressionable Conversations

Amanda Lytle

Sit down. Be quiet. Stop talking. Quit asking questions. People think you're too much. Got it. While I was trying to play it cool after receiving this feedback from a *friend* during a coffee date turned "here's how to be a more socially acceptable person" workshop that I hadn't signed up for, my emotions were busy taking form as a lump in my throat big enough to choke on. Imagine having your personality critiqued, your level of energy questioned, and your voice squashed when you thought you were just grabbing a cup of coffee to catch up with a new friend. There I was, in Melbourne, Australia, November 2012, a few weeks into my one-way ticket adventure to the land down under, thinking I was doing an amazing job of meeting new friends and socializing as I explored this new city. In actuality, it felt like I was being steamrolled by the social police. Feeling mortified that anyone would think I was annoying because of how engaged I was in social settings, I did my best to look past the emotional devastation of that dreadful conversation to find the positive. I genuinely wanted people in my presence to feel heard. I wanted people to feel safe speaking to me. I wanted people to know how deeply I cared about their experiences. What's a girl to do when she is passionate, curious, empathetic, and unapologetically conversational? Welcome to *The Safe Haven* podcast. I am your host, Amanda Lytle.

It didn't quite happen overnight, though. The next step after that life-altering scenario in Melbourne took place during some very cold, dark days in early 2019. This time of year in Haliburton, Ontario, already has limited daylight hours and tends to be the kind of cold that creeps up your spine and seeps outward and into your muscles. The extra darkness came from having just ended a very significant intimate relationship. For numerous reasons, he was just not the one for me. My inner knowing had pulled away from the relationship much earlier, but I tried to reflect in every way on what I could do better, how I could try harder, and how I could be more adaptive. In the end, we just didn't match, and I grieved hard! For someone who feels as deeply as I do, I was broken. I knew deep down that I was doing the best things for me and for him in the long run, but the dark days spent overthinking the "what ifs" and "maybes" and cold nights of sleeping alone felt like they'd never end.

Being an avid podcast listener already, I started exploring a few with this newfound time to myself. I fell into one in particular in which the host was raw and real about her emotions as well as what she was experiencing in a very public breakup. I cried when she cried. I laughed when she laughed. The relatability and parallels I found between her emotions and mine made me feel less alone, especially when she talked about how she knew she had done the right thing. She was sharing everything I was feeling in a very vulnerable (and public!) way, emphasizing the harsh reality that the pain was part of the journey when you really love someone. I felt that to my bones. As the weeks went by, she healed, and I did too. I found strength in her perspectives and often found myself reading articles she mentioned and listening to podcasts she found helpful. Although we were on our own paths and didn't know one another personally, we were together, which was such a powerful realization. Connection to messages and feeling less alone was attainable in an audio format, where hosts and listeners are connected on a level that's so unique. I started to draw conclusions about the importance of community in this space and sharing courageously in a public and vulnerable way.

The final reaffirming moment before the official creation of *The Safe Haven* happened in May 2019. A large group of my closest friends were coming together at my family's cottage for my thirty-first birthday. One of my best friends, Jess, was organizing the majority of it and simply asked me for a list of the people I'd love to have there. Keeping it traditional to the girls' weekends we've had in the past, I created a long list of my closest girlfriends and people I admired most that were within a day's drive. These were the people I knew would appreciate the gathering of big hearts and great minds in a beautiful century-old cottage on the lake with a breathtaking view. The list had more than thirty-five names on it, making me emotional with gratitude, knowing how many of these women would do everything in their power to be there. As I was reflecting, I thought about the calibre of women that were going to be on this beautiful property, sharing stories and experiences, offering and receiving advice from other heart-driven beings. So many of these women had stories that would silence any room if shared, including huge successes, massive traumas, incredible losses, and beautiful recoveries. With a flashback to my "lesson" from the coffee shop seven years prior, it dawned on me how important it is to share these personal stories. It's in the sharing of these stories that subsequent crucial conversations are started and connections are made. It is how communities are created and how people can feel less alone. I couldn't drop the thought of starting a podcast. What if I created a space where people could share their stories? What if I could establish a community that encouraged and honoured vulnerability and speaking one's truth?

Today, I can be described as a person who chases their desires. Of course, there have been many times in my life that my limiting beliefs influenced my decisions, but there was such a strong pull into the world of podcasting that I just had to trust the process and go for it.

Journaling has been a part of most of my adult life, coming and going when I need it most. It had proven to be a significant tool when overcoming limiting beliefs in the past, writing about successes and achievements as well as goals that I was working toward. This was another perfect time to keep going and to remind myself that perseverance in the past

It's in the sharing of these stories that subsequent crucial conversations are started and connections are made.

had proven successful. I knew I needed a few things in order to begin. I needed a name for the podcast. I needed to solidify the WHY behind it and clarify what this podcast was aiming to be. My soul was ignited just thinking about it, and the brainstorming began. I started a few Google docs: one with names of potential guests, one with a page for ideas, and another for listing my values and feelings I wanted my guests, and myself, to experience in this space. Two nights before my birthday, on the night of May 8, 2019, I crawled into bed with a racing mind. Staring at the ceiling, I allowed my emotions to ride the waves. I was doubting my abilities while visualizing my podcast in the top charts. I was telling myself I didn't have a following large enough to push my podcast into success while feeling excitement about the conversations I would be a part of. I was wondering if I had the time for this project while imagining it as my only source of income. I just needed a name. I quietly said out loud (to my late Grandma Lytle, to be honest!), "Please just send me something . . . anything that will help this get started." I'd hardly finished whispering when "The Safe Haven" came into my mind. I sat straight up in my bed with the biggest smile on my face and said thank you! That was it. I had the name, and *The Safe Haven* was officially on its way.

The morning of the ninth, I woke up early before my teaching day began so I could lock in the Gmail address and the Instagram handle to go with my newfound podcast name. It was starting to feel real, and it'd been so long since I felt such momentum toward something so big. I could already see it growing and connecting people globally. Having travelled for a few years in my early twenties, having been a Rotary International Exchange Student[1] in 2005, and having spent a few years abroad, I was well-networked internationally and still maintained contact with many friends around the world. I knew I could count on my friends and family to help me make this become a reality! My birthday the year before had been in the middle of a pretty tumultuous time, so I'd promised myself that I'd at least exit my thirtieth year with a bang—and this was it!

My birthday is the tenth of May, and this was the day I started speaking and sharing about this endeavour with more clarity. I was communicating my ideas and vision without guarding the passion in my voice, and it was received really well with the few friends I had chosen to tell. I've spent the majority of my life making decisions for myself, then sharing them after I've made a commitment or a decision—in one case, even booking a one-way ticket to Australia! I always waited to share my news with others to avoid judgment and potential sway from the things I needed and wanted to do. Sometimes, however, and still to this day, there is a level of external processing and validation required for the decisions I make that involve other people. Deep down, I knew that I would be an ideal host for *The Safe Haven*, holding space for authenticity and vulnerability, and hearing my closest friends and family agree was the fuel I needed.

The next thing I needed to get rolling was a mic. An old friend from university named Cole was already hosting a hilarious and successful podcast. I knew he'd have some insights on how to get started, so I gave him a call. Not only did Cole have several suggestions for me, but he also offered his Blue Yeti mic to get me started! He sent it down to the girls' weekend with a mutual friend, Laura, from North Bay, Ontario, as she was already going to be making the drive. Things were lining up perfectly.

After playing around and doing some basic Google searches, I was getting familiar with the Yeti—what worked, what sounded best, and what I was up against for sound in my little family-owned cabin I was living in at the time. A Taurean to the core, I told myself I needed a nicer place like a recording studio and more professional gear to get rolling and be successful, but that niggling in my solar plexus told me I had this. Just keep going. By the end of May, I started inviting people over into my space or would join them in theirs, whichever felt the safest for them to share their story with me and our listeners. Week after week, I'd sit down with these incredible people, holding space and listening with intention while they shared a story of their choosing. It was picking up, and within five weeks I had an international audience and several hundred downloads! I must admit that my travel history and time abroad played a pivotal role in the spread of *The Safe Haven's* content around the world, and for that, I am forever grateful.

The summer of 2019 included a trip to the UK, a road trip across Canada, then a month in Bali. Between my return from the UK and arrival in British Columbia, something happened with the mic, but I wasn't aware of just how detrimental that was until I went to play back the recording with another university friend, Carolyn, that we'd recorded during my stop in Winnipeg. Carolyn shared the story about her son's diagnosis with infant leukemia. When I arrived in BC and had time to edit that recording, I learned that about eight minutes into it, static took over and the recording was ruined. I was devastated and extremely embarrassed. I'd messed up, and I didn't know or fully understand how. Before reaching back out to Carolyn, I tried everything I could to salvage the lost recording. Nothing. I was going to have to rerecord. Carolyn was incredibly understanding and was actually looking forward to the opportunity to rerecord! Her son's health was improving, and by the time I was going to be driving back across the country, he would have been wrapping up his final round of chemo! I exhaled with the deepest appreciation and gratitude, and I felt relief that her sweet son's journey had taken a fabulous turn to the positive! This lesson also served as a reminder that I am, in fact, a human. Things happen. Perfectionism is unattainable and crushes dreams, but that is no reason to give up.

I'd never felt so passionate about any other project in my life as I did about this podcast. My listeners were still listening weekly, and many had reached out for updates from my travels and what was going on in my own life, so at this point in my podcasting adventure, I'd started recording a solo episode weekly and named those releases "TGIT: Thank Goodness it's Thursday!" It started to take off, and friends were loving the weekly updates on my life and my travels. Without a reliable mic, I improvised, recording these solo episodes with my Apple headphones and my Macbook Pro, often sitting alone in my car or on my bed. Even while in Bali, I used my trusty Apple headphones to record three times with guests, twice attaching the Apple headphones to the Yeti mic with hair elastics to improvise, and once hanging them from a canopy bed between Lindsey's face and mine while we recorded about her head injury. It did the trick, and *The Safe Haven* continued!

I knew I needed to get better and more reliable equipment. Having travelled for most of the summer and trying to get settled in BC with a teaching job, funds were tight. I knew deep down that I needed to make the investment, so I began doing some research. I settled on the vibe I wanted to go with, first. I wanted to be able to sit comfortably, across from my guest, without holding onto anything. I pictured another best friend, also named Jess, and me, sitting in her living room. Jess was sitting on her couch, and I was sitting, covered in a blanket, on the beanbag chair on her floor. I knew immediately that mic stands were in order, the kind that could be at different heights and angles. Now, I just needed to go buy the mic stands, the mics, the recording device, and the headphones to monitor sound.

I committed in September of that year and was completely blown away by the quality change in the sound production. With the new equipment, I needed to also start editing in something other than what my laptop provided. I used a basic free program, and with practice and time, I started to get much better at the entire production process, doing everything myself.

I drove back to Ontario in January 2020, stopping in Winnipeg to rerecord with Carolyn. Back in Ontario, I started lining up recordings with people all over the province, committing myself to weekends away to record multiple episodes at a time to acquire content to edit over the next few months. It was early in February, and I was settling back into my weekly routine of teaching during the day and editing every evening besides Mondays. When I'm within a quick drive from Mama's house, I join her and Papa for dinner, then Mama and I dive into watching *The Bachelor* or *The Bachelorette*. (Mama and Papa are my grandparents!) We've done it for years, and it's always been such a special night, and one that I look forward to. One early February evening had a fun spin to it. During a commercial break, something about a podcast network flashed across the screen. Mama and Papa have one of those fancy things that allows you to rewind your TV, so I asked if we could rewatch that commercial. I had no idea at the time what a podcast network was, but I knew immediately that I was going to be emailing them when I got home that night. My goal was to reach out and establish connections with other podcasters and potential guests, so I was feeling really optimistic about this opportunity!

A few days later, I got a reply, and the team at Frequency Podcast Network wanted me to jump on a call with them later the following Friday, if possible. I had no idea what I was in for, but I committed to the call on the spot. Our call that Friday was nearly an hour long, and they seemed really impressed and excited about where *The Safe Haven* was heading. I still didn't quite comprehend what a podcast network was, but it sounded exciting. As the call was wrapping up, one of the team members started talking about a sales team, and my heart sank. There's the catch. I knew it. I wanted to clarify what this would mean for me, so I sheepishly asked, "So, you mentioned a sales team . . . what is this going to cost me?" With smiles in their voices, they said that I wouldn't have to pay anything! They were hoping to work hard to help me get paid!

An infinite number of things changed in March 2020 with the arrival of COVID-19, which meant that I needed to change things up quickly to adjust to the fact that I would no longer be able to record in person with my guests. I started to explore virtual spaces for recording, trying everything from FaceTime Audio to Instagram's video chat, and I ultimately settled very happily on Zoom as my primary virtual meeting space. Along with some adjustments in podcasting, there were some fundamental changes and deep dives that were necessary in my own life, which were highlighted on May 25, 2020, with the murder of George Floyd. Along with many others, I welcomed the opportunity to really reevaluate the platform I was creating and who it represented, and I made some crucial pivots to enhance the community I intended to be for everyone. The work of anti-racism continues daily, and the learning and unlearning will never cease. I admit that I've made many mistakes, but I know now that when I make them, they're less likely to be made out of ignorance and more out of pure effort to do better. I can always do better in this space, and I will never stop trying to be more inclusive.

The year rolled on, and my podcast and I packed our bags and moved across the country in the summer of 2020. Having a podcast that could be recorded remotely allowed me to really increase the size of my guest list, and I was able to focus on the little things that enhanced sound quality. With sound quality improving came more opportunities, and I was so grateful to the Frequency Podcast Network for their help getting me my first paid sponsorship opportunity! I would be getting paid to insert ads into my podcast for a set number of weeks as a campaign and would even be paid a host fee for having it on my podcast and reading the ads myself. This felt like such a victory, so you can imagine how deflated I felt in November when I was cc'ed in an email I shouldn't have been. It was a complete accident, but the "Hi Amanda" at the beginning was intended for a different Amanda on the team. There were some very analytical numbers and opinions in this long thread of emails, which I read thoroughly because the email was to "Amanda." I sent a text to the sender to let her know it'd been received and that I was curious about what it all meant for the future of *The Safe Haven*. The numbers I was seeing were showing a lack of growth, and I was feeling extremely discouraged with the contrast of these numbers to my level of love and passion for this podcast. Was this the beginning of the end? Her reply was extremely apologetic and laced with a tone of embarrassment. I shouldn't have seen that email. It was intended for another Amanda on the team and was all in preparation for a more concise presentation and meeting to be had with me and one other person in a few short weeks to discuss what 2021 should look like for

The Safe Haven. I was able to transition into a place of excitement and intention after working through my emotions and feeling torn and anxious about what was to come. I really had to sit with the idea that my passion project might not be what I believed it was, but the other side of that felt like a really supported climb ... one I was tying up my shoes for and ready to tackle with a really deep desire to succeed.

I couldn't let go of the feelings I experienced when I'd hear someone gush about the podcast, or about how listeners and guests were connecting online or in person. Pre-COVID, my friend Michelle told me about how people walked up to her on the main street of Haliburton, thanking her for sharing her story and hugging her! She still laughs to this day about it because one woman threw her arms around Michelle, and Michelle didn't even know who it was. My friend Danielle shared her two incredibly different birth stories on the podcast, which led to a packed inbox of messages from women reaching out to share their experiences with hospital births and home births, asking questions and thanking her for speaking so vulnerably. That, my friends, is connection, empathy, and relatability. I felt so sure of *The Safe Haven*, and even more so every time I received positive feedback. The more deeply I understood the effects this podcast was having on others, the more deeply I understood the reason this podcast needed to continue. The world was buzzing around me, and the filtered squares of people's lives online with thousands of likes and comments seemed to minimize my skewed perceptions of success. I was associating a large following with immediate success in the world of podcasting. What I didn't realize then, but have realized since, is that my definition of success had become directly related to numbers. I was chasing numbers of listens and downloads, dynamic ad insertion inventory, and followers on Instagram. Even though I was still heading into every conversation heart first, my head was still wrapped up in the connection of statistics defining success. I'd forgotten that showing up consistently week after week was a form of success. Holding space for authenticity, creativity, and in-depth conversations was a form of success. Helping people feel less alone and nurturing a space where relatability is real was a form of success, and these were the forms of success that I was responsible for creating. My guests and I were joining people on their walks and runs, keeping them company while they ran errands or worked around the house, sitting with them in waiting rooms or during hospital treatments, and riding with them during their road trips. These were the callings to dig deep. These were the reasons I needed to find my courage to use my voice and keep moving forward when problems presented themselves. These were the things I needed to focus on while shapeshifting *The Safe Haven* into the new year.

Allowing myself a few days to digest the analysis email I'd received about the podcast was key before a short meeting I had with the network's team afterward. We discussed what *The Safe Haven* and I were doing well, and what slight changes could mean moving forward. Podcast meeting notes in hand about a slight change in direction, I was feeling re-ignited. *The Safe Haven* wasn't dying after all, it just needed some refining and redirection. I knew what I had to do going into 2021, and a few simple things could really make a difference. I carried this new knowledge into my December recordings, which I planned on having as my January releases. This new intel solidified the intention with which I prepared and even spoke to my guests before recording. The new framework was going to surround a takeaway message for the listeners in twenty-five to thirty minutes, as opposed to my previously longer recordings and conversations. The goal was to dive into a life challenge or event that changed the guest's life, and what it was that they did in order to keep moving forward. After a few recordings in this new and very intentional format, I was elated. The bonus I didn't even think about at the time was that I had nearly halved my editing time. I was able to pump out great content and, in turn, had more time to find new guests and have more incredible conversations.

In my thirty-three years on this planet, I can truly say I've never experienced a ride or a rush like I do with this podcast. Everything *The Safe Haven* entails is a form of self-care for me, but it's also proven to be one of my greatest teachers. It's taught me about the importance of consistency more than anything else in my life. It's helped me understand that I can leave a mark and create an impact on others. It's proven that numbers don't equal success. This podcast has helped me overcome limiting beliefs by keeping my soul ignited and craving more.

A guest I had earlier this year told me about a quote from Humble the Poet about finding and chasing your obsession, not just your passion. Passions come and go, but an obsession will last. I'm sure if you've had any sort of passion project turned obsession, you can wholeheartedly relate to this feeling. I've found my obsession with *The Safe Haven*, and the growth of this podcast is in my hands. And my heart. I see the work this podcast is doing! It's starting crucial and critical conversations, and it's helping people feel less alone. Do I make mistakes and say things I shouldn't say? Absolutely I do, but I am doing my best to lead from a place of love, and growth needs friction and discomfort at times. I'm committed to that.

I wouldn't be where I am today without the constant love and support from my family and closest friends—the collective "you can do this!" energy that they constantly provide me with when I try something new: book a one-way ticket to the other side of the world, drive across the country alone in the winter, start a photography business, take new courses online, start a podcast from the ground up, or contribute a chapter to an incredible book series!

To my best friends and family: I can't articulate how grateful I am for our friendships, conversations, and time together, even if it's via FaceTime and from different time zones. You add so much value to my life and inspire me daily.

Born and raised in Minden, Ontario, Amanda Lytle has always had her mind set on the world. She is an intensely dynamic woman with an infectious passion for humanity. She's vibrant and compassionate. She's the friend you want walking by your side in times of great joy and in times of  sorrow because she never makes the moment her own. She is the rock any friend dreams of leaning on.

From her teenage years onward, Amanda has chased her dreams while actively crossing items off her bucket list. Amanda is not one to sit back and watch. Instead, she embraces new experiences and challenges. Her curiosity fuels her love of learning, which is endless.

Not only does she offer this support to friends and family, she also gives it to her students. Amanda is a teacher of many things. Whether she is teaching yoga, high school, or podcasting workshops, she teaches with grace and an open heart. Amanda cherishes her relationships. No matter where she is in the world or how busy she is, she always has time for the special people in her life and is excellent at communicating her love for them.

The newest addition to Amanda's passion-filled life is her podcast, *The Safe Haven*. She has opened her arms and welcomed guests from all walks of life. Her podcast uplifts in every sense. It uplifts the raw, vulnerable messages of her guests. It uplifts listeners from all over the globe. It uplifts herself by paving purpose in her life. She is making change for the better in each episode, and the journey has just begun.

Chapter Seven

WAKE-UP CALLING

Jane Middlehurst

If 2020 had a theme, mine would be this: the phoenix rising from a dumpster fire.

The Rug

So, you know that really pivotal moment in life when you're going along with life as you know it and suddenly the "rug is pulled out" from under you? That's exactly the dumpster-fire feeling I'm talking about here. It is how my 2020 went down, with the cherry on the top being the abrupt end of my ten-year relationship. I know that 2020 was challenging for so many of us, but for me, it brought on healing from childhood trauma and the big breakup. I saw none of it coming. But having a head's up wouldn't have made a difference. As it turns out, the lessons and gifts we discover in our so-called "dumpster-fire seasons" are more powerful because of the fact that we see none of it coming. And that is what it means to truly come into contact with our raw humanness—what it means to be a human being in this messy life.

Throughout the past few years, I had been focusing on professional development. I had pursued coaching professionally, I had completed two coach training programs, and I was starting to build out my coaching practice. Then 2020 came in with other plans that pushed my plans to the backseat.

Haunting Ghosts

Lots of big and little events that year began triggering the deep child-hood wound of my mom's passing, but I was asleep to it and the impact it was having on me, my life, my work, and in my relationships. I knew I wasn't coping well, as I tried desperately to help a family member in addiction recovery, but my attempts to help her find herself again led to me losing myself completely. As each one of my boundaries blurred and then broke, I bargained with myself, believing that bending my boundaries was okay so long as it was for the greater good. I would sacrifice myself in the short term to save another in the long term.

The thing is that I know better. No one can save anyone, but I convinced myself that I could, that I was strong enough, resilient enough, and ready enough. I could take this issue on in the name of love. But addiction recovery is not something you strong-arm someone into, no matter how much you love them. I'd been down this road three times before with the same family member over the course of twenty years, and what continues to become clearer and clearer to me is that addiction is a hungry ghost that haunts its victims, leaves a massive path of destruction in its wake, and robs people of their worth, life, and relationships.

The tight grip of addiction is ruthless and painful, and it renders you powerless, even as a helpless bystander. Addiction stops at nothing and doesn't care who it takes out as long as it's being fed. This reality was a lesson I relearned in 2020, only this time it came attached with the surfacing of my unhealed childhood wounds.

It wasn't clear to me at the time, but professional development is directly connected to personal reflection, growth, and (sometimes) healing. I had spent a considerable amount of time growing professionally, but I hadn't noticed the inner work that was still needed for personal growth.

Feel Your Feels

Childhood-trauma healing. Wait, why? How can I heal from an event I can't change? My mom dying when I was eight years old was definitely a trauma, but how was it affecting me now? What could I even do about it? Turns out, everything. I was unaware I was carrying around my unhealed childhood wounds, and I was equally as unaware of how they were affecting every facet of my life. Like, whoa. And, at the same

What became clear [...] is that life is a mirror that reflects what we carry on the inside.

time, I had so much self-compassion during this discovery for what I didn't realize and tend to. Self-compassion was a muscle I had to build within, and it was a bumpy ride. Sometimes I was really good at it, and other times not so much. I had to learn to be fresh in the moment, to meet each moment and be with whatever was there: doubt, self-criticism, shame, self-aversion, and anxiety, and I had to hold it with compassion and just let it be.

What became clear to me in 2020 is that life is a mirror that reflects what we carry on the inside. Who we are, how we are, how we go about the world, our relationships, our work, they are all a reflection of what we hold onto deeply and tightly on the inside. So, yes, that means inner work including healing wounds, core beliefs, and the cycles we repeat until we're ready and willing to face ourselves, dig in, and do the work that frees us.

What also became clear to me during this time was how masterful we are at rejecting (or just not seeing) our wounds or parts of our story that are too painful to hold onto compassionately. It's no wonder we develop ways of coping by cutting ourselves off from pain, by disconnecting from it, but as I discovered, doing so also disconnects us from healing and thriving.

Trees Grow Up and Down

Truthfully, I had no idea I needed to do this inner healing work. I consider myself a self-development junkie, always looking at learning the next thing. Self-improvement, check. Self-leadership, check. Self-awareness, check. But self-awareness, as I came to discover, meant way more than what I considered.

Here's a metaphor I came up with during this time:

Trees grow up toward the sun, branches reaching and growing stronger. We see that trees grow up. And in a similar way, we could say that our self-development is how we grow up. As a tree grows up, it also grows down, its root system expanding and getting stronger to support the tree above ground. This "growing down" is necessary for the tree to "grow up." It's a both/and scenario that supports the overall growth of a tree. So, if our self-development is how we grow up, then our self-awareness and inner work is how we grow down. We grow down when we go beneath the surface and tend to deep roots of healing. Just like a tree, our growth happens when we grow UP and DOWN. Our challenge is to remember the roots when all we notice is the tree.

Our challenge is to remember the roots when all we notice is the tree.

From Ground Zero

The catalyst of my big breakup came the moment I "face-planted" on the proverbial floor because really, there's nowhere but up from there. The beauty in this moment was not immediate; it was hard fought and hard earned. The knee-jerk reaction in a moment of complete despair is to want to collapse in on yourself, to shrink, to question your value and worth. It's not easy to see anything but the dust and debris of a life you once lived. But from the floor, as you lie there wondering what you're going to do to pull yourself together again, you begin to notice the unique vantage point you have—yes, even with your face on the floor.

As the dust settles and you're looking around at all these broken pieces, you get this glimpse of hope and a renewed sense of self starting to peek through. You think, *My God, maybe this was all meant to burn down this way so that I could carve a new path forward that I couldn't have done otherwise.* See, wisdom arrives to you. Wisdom is not an inspirational quote you read. Wisdom arrives in the spaciousness you allow. Wisdom needs a breath of air to float in and land on you. In this moment, I realized that all my self-development and inner work couldn't carry me much further without the total collapse of my life as it were. It was the wake-up call I so desperately needed but was so blissfully unaware of.

Gifts-From-Floor Moments

From the floor, I had no choice but to see myself and my life for exactly what it was. During the breakup, I noticed as each of my illusions vanished before my eyes. Whatever I was unwilling to acknowledge pre-breakup made itself crystal clear during the breakup. Here is where I found myself on my knees, palms turned up in surrender to whatever was calling me forward. I got real with myself here, like really real, because there was no wiggling out of this gracefully—it was about the grit before the grace.

In this moment, everything that needed my attention came rushing forward. I wasn't just faced with one thing, I was faced with many all at once. This moment was blinding and defeating, yet it was the exact thing I needed to see. If life is a reflection of our inner world, then this moment was the equivalent of me stuck in a house of mirrors I couldn't find my way out of until I really looked around and found my way. But the way out was to go within.

I saw so clearly how I had not been standing in my power, my worth, and my truth. I noticed how although I had taken the last few years to pursue a new career choice and had focused deeply on my self-development, I hadn't noticed all the ways that old patterns were still hanging around, something that had everything to do with my personal and professional development, my work, my relationships, and my life. The interesting thing is that life knows what lessons you need and keeps serving them to you until you pay attention and dive in. Same lesson, different cast, different scene, different script—but same ol' lesson in disguise.

I was chatting with a friend not long after I started coming up from the floor. I was starting to feel the power of receiving these hard-earned gifts, and I said, "You know, this is how resilience is born and how you stand in your worth and your power. You don't get these things from eating bonbons on the couch on a Sunday. I mean, I've had plenty of Sundays like that, but that's not how my Sundays are right now, and I realize that this is a 'just for now' thing, and it won't always be this way. I'm proud of myself and these hard-earned gifts."

Becoming resilient, finding your power, standing in your worth, and having complete faith—these are not things that come from easy times, they are born from the times your spirit is tested and you decide to rise.

Brave Rising

My rising season happened pretty quickly. It's hard to explain the stark contrast in the shift from my floor moment to the very next moment of rising the fuck up. I remember feeling shocked by how quickly this shift happened, because let's be honest: when you're down and out like that, you can't really see the forest for the trees, nothing makes sense,

... bravery is an act of courage. You don't wait for bravery to arrive because it never does.

and you've got no clue what your next steps might be.

What I did know was that any moment I felt a nudge of momentum, I moved with it. I became as comfortable as anyone can be with being uncomfortable and not having all the answers. I got friendly with living in the grey area of life and moving from one moment to the next. I developed deep faith and trust as a result of allowing myself to take control of my life but also loosen the grip on how it was all going down. I let go in every sense of the word but held on tightly to myself. I had my own back, and I became "my person" after losing the person I thought was my person. I got me.

It's not lost on me the irony that my Instagram account name is @brave.rising. I created this account a few years ago and chose the name in the spirit of inspiring myself and others to rise bravely as we step more and more into ourselves, our truth, our inner work, our path in life, and our unique wish to contribute/serve the world around us. I realized back then that bravery is not cheerleading your way through scary moments, that bravery is not an inspirational quote like "you got this, girl!" Instead, bravery is an act of courage. You don't wait for bravery to arrive because it never does. You gain bravery by facing your fears, being scared and unsure, and doing the thing anyway. You feel brave when you reach the other side of your journey after walking that courageous path. Anything leading up to that feels like shaking in your boots, wobbly next steps, and being unsure of the outcome. Taking the risk is betting on yourself against all odds and knowing that even if you lose, you'll still be rewarded with gifts from lessons learned as you step into your next try. There is no losing, only gaining.

> **You feel brave when you reach the other side of your journey after walking that courageous path.**

You Hold the Pen

So, there I was in 2020, in the midst of a career transition from the corporate world to coaching. I was wrapping up the first of two intense coach training programs. I was feeling pretty good about my path forward and was excited about how my coaching business would take off. And then 2020 happened, and it took me down and out.

Life has interesting ways of helping you along your path. So, on reflection, it's fitting that my 2020 was a huge invitation to GROW through what I was GOING through. Here was my own brave rising season that eventually led to me writing my brave new beginning.

Anchors and Pillars

In the midst of everything I was GROWING through, I got clear on things I now consider my anchors. An anchor holds you steady in place; it's how you stay rooted in yourself. It can reflect your values and intentions, your moral compass, your way of coming back home to yourself. It can be all these things and more. Remember the tree metaphor? After digging deep and tending to my roots, I discovered some key things that had been missing from my life, and what was missing became my anchors. They are:

Self-Acceptance

The ability to accept myself as I am right now in this moment without judgment, ridicule, or harsh backlashing for whatever reason I invent. The ability to accept myself as a growing, changing, evolving, messy person simply being human. To honour the range of emotions, thoughts, and experiences through this sometimes messy life and know that they all belong, and that I belong as well.

Self-Compassion

The ability to be gentle with myself as I move through tough times. The tendency in these moments is to get down on myself. As Tara Brach[1] explains, mindful presence is like two wings of a bird. The first wing is acceptance (of what is), or what we think of when we think of mind-fulness—being aware of our thoughts, emotions, and current situation and accepting simply what is by allowing it and not pushing it away or rejecting. The other wing of mindful presence is compassion, which is how we bring tender, gentle, loving care to those moments. Without compassion, we have awareness and acceptance of what is but we can't meet it with the gentleness these hard moments need. When we are willing to sit with ourselves, sit with what is, sit with uncomfortable truths, then we become more aware and more mindful, something that can be painful if we forget to bring that other wing, the wing of self-compassion. We need doses and doses of self-compassion.

Self-Belief

The ability to have unshakable belief in myself to get through tough times and to achieve what I want to achieve going forward. Holding the belief that I already have everything I need inside me to weather tough storms and carry out any vision I want to bring to fruition. The big issue here is noticing what we already have and leveraging it forward rather than noticing all that we seemingly lack. Our brains are wired with a negativity bias, which means that when we are not distracted with "human doing"—to-do lists, projects, doing all the things—and we return to "human being" with whatever is present inside ourselves, our brains default to negativity, something you'll notice as inner critic or bully self-talk. This self-talk is self-defeating steeped in comparison. It is feelings of not being good enough, and it seeks external validation. The shift came for me when I noticed it happening, so I started seeking internal validation and cultivating the attitude that *I've already got this, I can do this, and there's no reason why I can't.* You're the best cheerleader you'll ever have if you let yourself be one.

Self-Trust

The ability to have my own back and lean on myself, knowing that I am my very own best friend. To check in with myself first, always. When we honour our inner wisdom and intuition about the direction in which we want to move, even when it may not make sense to others, we develop a deep sense of self-trust. It is to know when we feel off course and trust ourselves enough to abandon what feels off, to course-correct, then move in a direction that feels right. It is deep trust in knowing that no matter what happens, I got me. And you got you too.

These are the main values that became anchors for me through my grow-through-what-you-go-through season, but I can't go without mentioning the PILLARS that helped stand me up and set my life in a new direction. If anchors keep me steady, rooted, and coming back home to myself, then pillars elevate me, hold me higher, and help me reach where I want to go. Here are my pillars:

Wholehearted Living

Brené Brown describes wholehearted living like this: "Wholehearted living is about engaging in our lives from a place of worthiness. It means cultivating the courage, compassion, and connection to wake up in the morning and think, *No matter what gets done and how much is left undone, I am enough.* It's going to bed at night thinking, *Yes, I am imperfect and vulnerable and sometimes afraid, but that doesn't change the truth that I am also brave and worthy of love and belonging.*"[2] For me, wholehearted living means all of this plus leading my life by honouring my whole heart, no half measures. It is to meet my heart's deepest longings in how I wish to show up in this world.

Powerful Relationships

In my grow-through-what-you-go-through season, every single one of my relationships deepened, especially the relationship I have with myself. I saw how sometimes I had been getting in my own way or dismissing relationships that didn't seem to "meet me" where I was. From a different perspective, I pinpointed this down to getting in my own way, and that's not to say that there are people we gel with and people we won't, that's just the simple truth in life. Once you have these face-on-floor moments, your walls come tumbling down, humility makes a grand entrance, and you soften to what people can really offer you in their own unique way as well as how they can lift you up. I also got really good at leaning on people in this time, which is something I never would have done before. The thing is, we don't have to go at life alone. Many times we think our messy human experience doesn't belong or that we don't belong and that we should only present the version of ourselves that shows the world that we have our shit together. But this is not what cultivates true, deep connections within ourselves and with others. When we show ourselves vulnerable, we let people see that we all struggle, we all have messy moments, and we all rise. We dispel the myth that we don't belong and that we are alone. When we show our humanness, we give other people two things: the inspiration and courage for them to do the same and the safety required to make that happen. I began to see each relationship and each person with the unique power they naturally bring to life, and from here I borrowed their strengths, their power, and their gifts to help me rise, but I could only do it by first showing myself vulnerably.

Connection to Myself

We think we know ourselves, but if we're honest, there's a lot we are unaware of, which isn't a judgment. Sometimes, we just haven't woken up to some hard truths, and often times (most times), we are masters of not seeing ourselves. Our brains are masterful at self-deception in order to keep us safe, protected, and small. Our brains are efficient machines, but if we learn to bring ourselves into the equation and interrupt the machine-like way we go about life, what we discover is that the "machine" can no longer be on autopilot when we bring our soul into the mix. Bringing your soul means developing a deep connection with yourself, knowing who you are, how you are—both the smooth and rough edges—knowing what values you hold, what dreams and desires you aspire to, and honouring all of it. Notice the machine-like ways about yourself, then interrupt the machine by consciously bringing your soul. Connection to myself was where I began to feel that I belonged, not only to myself but also as myself, in my business. I took my seat at the table and owned my place because I had a true sense of belonging.

Perfectly Imperfect

I'm not perfect and perfection was never the goal, but on reflection, it would seem that "being perfect" or being "perfectly ready" were the things that held me back. Of course, perfection was an unconscious driver, and if you had asked me, I would've denied it. But the truth is that I was endlessly striving for something, but that "something" was a moving target I could never achieve. When I started showing my messy human experience to others, when I was vulnerable because there was no other way to be, and when I let others see all my imperfections by openly talking bravely about them, that is when I felt really REAL, really accepted, and really ready. The irony. You can't skip the messy middle because that's where you discover all the gifts, and that is where

I learned that taking messy imperfect action in my business was the path that got me furthest. When I tried to show up as anything other than myself, I noticed that it was unfulfilling and didn't draw potential clients in the same way I experienced when I was my true self, messy and all.

Just Take Your Seat

In my corporate career, I worked with individuals, groups, and teams on leadership development and coaching. Often, these sessions would be in a group format in some boardroom. Picture it: U-shaped table, chairs around it, and packages in front of each seat with materials for the session. As the leader of these sessions, I was the first in the room, and through many years of sessions, I observed many different ways people entered the room. There were the people who were the early birds who sat at the front and couldn't wait to get started and participate in every damn thing. There were the latecomers who didn't give a hoot about the session and were there because they were mandated to be, and their only concern was what we were having for lunch. There were the "Nervous Nellies" who feared being spotlighted or called out in any way during the session. And there were the skeptics with folded arms sending "don't mess with me" vibes. It was these people I coined "snipers." Their entire purpose of being in session was to derail it. You know the type: the person who asks a question just to cause friction, to shoot holes in theories, or to just challenge you or others. Being in leadership development and coaching gave me so much insight into human behaviour. It was wild. Even just the way someone entered a room revealed so much.

I experimented with many ways of inviting people into a session because I like to try new things and observe what happens. One day I decided on a truly empowering way to welcome in a bunch of new/first-time leaders in the organization. I welcomed them in the usual way and watched as they poured their coffee, grabbed a cookie or granola bar, then chose their seat, but my opener was much different. Instead of saying, "Welcome to x, y, z session, blah, blah, blah," I said, "Welcome to this session. You've chosen your seat, but I want you to really TAKE YOUR SEAT. Own your seat here at this table. You belong here." And that was how I started one of the most empowering leadership sessions I've ever led. Just that one shift in my introduction shifted everything for these first-time leaders who felt wobbly in their new roles.

In the same way, I realized that I hadn't yet taken my seat in my coaching business. I hadn't claimed my spot or raised my hand to say THIS IS WHO I AM. I kept myself general, vague, and hidden in the back of the room. I was undecided, not ready (excuse!), and was waiting for permission from someone other than myself. The moment I realized this truth, I dropped my excuses and just took my damn seat!

Belonging

Much of my journey has been the tension between belonging and not belonging. I noticed this tension in myself and in others all around me. It seemed as if no one was immune to a sense of whether they belonged. At first, I thought it was just me, but I noticed more and more how this sense of belonging came up in coaching conversations with clients and in coaching circles where coaches from all over the world came together to chat "coachy" things.

Each person who crossed my path in some way, shape, or form wrestled with a sense of belonging. Some examples of statements I heard include: "I don't belong because I'm not like them; I don't belong because I'm not ready yet; I don't belong because I need to get this certificate or degree first; I don't belong because I don't have enough experience yet and no one would take me seriously; I don't belong because I'm not like them and I do things differently; I don't belong because I'm too young; I don't belong because there's something missing in me and what if they find out?" The list could go on and on.

What you may notice in this list is a theme of "them versus me," which actually keeps each of us separate and apart. And most of these justifications are unfounded and untrue. But I noticed that when people spoke bravely about their sense of *not* belonging, it was the EXACT thing that led them to feeling a sense of belonging. When we speak our truth, we connect to one another; that's just how it works. Because here's the thing: belonging or not belonging is a universal experience no matter what details colour our experience. Whatever is keeping you feeling a sense of not belonging, speak it bravely and authentically, and I bet you will find a connection and a sense of belonging that you've been craving.

And here's the bigger thing that happens when you share parts of yourself bravely, the parts that make you feel like you don't belong: you actually cultivate a deep sense of belonging to yourself by showing up as yourself with wobbly knees and sweaty palms. We tend to wait with bated breath to be accepted INTO whatever we deem as being outside of us. We tend to shapeshift into who we think we should be, or we armour up to protect our true self. But the truth is that in our waiting to be accepted, we sacrifice ourselves and true belonging. But if we can pause and find our way back INTO ourselves, anchoring into our truth and showing up as ourselves, we come to learn that the roots of belonging actually begin with belonging to ourselves first.

Jane Middlehurst is a Certified Integral Coach® and transformational coach who supports leaders, coaches, creatives, and sensitives in expressing their unique calling in life and work. Often, this transformational work comes during a transition season in life, is guided by developmental growth within ourselves, and sits at the edge of our wobbly "what's next." This is the work of the brave who dare to lead a wholehearted life and, in many ways, leave the world a better place. Jane has spent more than fifteen years studying human development and designing custom leadership development programs and retreats for Canadian Fortune 500 companies. Her work has been deeply fulfilling and enriching; however, everything changed when she left an unhealthy corporate environment. During this transition season, she was reminded of how the Vikings would burn their boats on the shores of distant lands as a sign of "no going back" — they went all in. In this way, Jane "burned the boats" on her former career and went all in on the shores of her new coaching land. She bravely forged a new path by trusting her intuition to answer her deepest calling and now helps others do the same. Today, Jane guides people in the power of their true being, helping them rise bravely into leading their brightest vision. Jane offers one-on-one custom coaching programs as well as team and group programs.

Chapter Eight

One Person Can Make a Difference

Jessica Danford

The year was 2015. I was constipated, struggling with IBS, joint and skin problems, fertility issues, thyroid and blood sugar irregularities, and low iron, among other various and seemingly unrelated symptoms. My medical team kept testing me for mono, but there was no sign of kissy lips to be found. This was also the year my youngest sister and I were both diagnosed with celiac disease. I had been hounding my doctor to test me for celiac disease based on symptoms I had experienced since childhood and family medical history I was aware of; however, I was always dismissed.

So, when my younger sister was hospitalized and diagnosed with the autoimmune disease, I was quickly sent for a colonoscopy and endoscopy to confirm that I, too, was affected by celiac. For many, it is a devastating diagnosis, but for me, it was an expected one that I used to propel myself into a healthier life. I kept telling myself I wanted to build a wellness empire; I did not know what that looked like at the time, but I kept that thought in my mind. I just knew I wanted to keep exploring wellness while motivating, inspiring, and empowering others along the way. It is funny how life works when you surrender to the process.

Six years later, having left my secure corporate job, I now run a virtual wellness community focused on those very principles that are continually evolving. I have become a published author, and most important and surprisingly, I have built an incredible awareness and advocacy passion project that has grown into directly helping families affected by food insecurity while on a gluten-free diet. I get asked a lot what I do, how I do it, and why I do it, and some days it is all a blur. To be honest, I'm not really sure what I am doing or how it will all fit together. I just keep pursuing the things that feel important to me, that light me up, and that give me the energy to keep going.

I fell in love with learning about the world and myself and really diving into who I wanted to be as a person.

Afflicted by trauma as a teen, I spent several years in a state of depression and addiction while living a vagrant life. At my lowest, one person handed me a piece of paper with a note stating where I could get some help, including some food. I swallowed my pride, took the help, then made a commitment to myself to take back my life and be the best me. That was a few years prior to my celiac diagnosis. I began making the hard choices and putting in the work to get my life back on track—mentally, financially, and spiritually, which included rebuilding my reputation as well as my relationships with others and myself. It took a lot of self-reflection and empowerment. But I did it. As I released my anger, fear, and shame from previous life experiences, I fell in love with learning about the world and myself and really diving into who I wanted to be as a person.

I started a blog in 2015 after being diagnosed with celiac disease. I had been sharing my meal creations on my personal Instagram and Facebook accounts and found that the people in my life had no interest in which gluten-free pasta I preferred or where the best gluten-free bread was to be found . . . because they did not eat gluten free!

The term "blogger" never resonated with me (my spelling and grammar skills are the reason autocorrect was created). I never saw myself as a writer, although at the advice of various therapists, counsellors, and my mom, I have journaled since a young age.

BLOG | blɒg |

NOUN

A regularly updated website or web page, typically run by an individual or small group, that is written in an informal or conversational style.

I initially partnered with my younger sister (who also has celiac disease) when I started the blog. It was a simple Instagram account to share the foods we were making along with the small businesses we found that supported people on a gluten-free diet. We called it Gfree-Wifey. We worked together on it for the first year until I fully took over the account.

I often get asked, what the heck is a Gfree-Wifey? Why do you call it that? Welp, the fear of internet trolls had me thinking I did not want to use my name, so I needed a brand name that could grow and adapt with me and my lifestyle.

G-free is short for gluten free. A person with celiac disease must maintain a strict gluten-free diet for life, so I knew "g-free" would age well, as it is a medically required lifelong diet I now had to follow.

Wifey – "Why 'wifey' when you're not married, Jess?" you might be wondering. Though I am not married, I respect the constructs of a relationship; in the same sense, I identify as wifey, not wife.

My sister and I felt the name was flexible enough to encompass various "wifey" perspectives; she was at home as a first-time mom navigating her new life and cooking gluten free for her family, while I was always out and about at restaurants and dinner parties. Together we covered it all—no matter what kind of wifey life people were living.

But the reason that wifey stuck and stayed after all these years is the definition from the Urban Dictionary:

WIFEY | ˈwʌɪfi |

NOUN (informal)

More special than a girlfriend. Different from a wife. The type of girl that's down for whatever. Your best friend/lover/partner in crime. That ride-or-die type chick. Has your back through anything and loves making you happy. All the perks without the actual marriage. A wifey is a good thing to be!

I was already a few years deep into my own personal empowerment journey, so the platform became more of a digital diary for me. It was my personal accountability tool to continue making healthy choices, and it pushed me to be creative in the kitchen by converting all my old classic recipes and favourites to gluten-free versions that were delicious. I was not only learning about the gluten-free diet, I was building a whole new skill set—working on photography, editing, lighting, writing, speaking, and showing up as a person who people trusted to share genuine gluten-free life experiences.

When the blog started, I was working full time in a career I had dedicated myself to with excellence after years of letting people down. I was doing all the right things, climbing the corporate ladder, and making amazing money. I worked hard to pull myself up and become the person I thought I was supposed to be, but what I was really doing was trading one addiction for another. My new addiction became work. "Work" was the place I could escape my reality, my problems, responsibilities, people, the world, everything. All I had to do was work. The problem is that I felt empty and unfulfilled. I was always unhappy and angry that I was working so hard for someone else to get rich, and it was literally helping no one.

Do you ever get that feeling that you don't know what you're supposed to be doing or that something big is about to happen, but you have no freaking idea what? That is me—constantly. I have all these ideas in my head, and when I'm not being true to myself, my beliefs and my personal code of ethics, I feel anxious, unhappy, and stressed. That's how I was feeling in my shallow job.

I was happily sharing my gluten-free adventures. I had my website built to house recipes, stories, events, and all the things I was doing every minute when I was not at work. However, I felt a disconnect—that feeling of unfulfillment creeping back in.

I am the worst blogger. Brands were messaging me, asking me to try their products and talk about them on my page. But here is the thing: I generally do not buy processed foods, so I was saying no thanks, even though the reason many people start a blog is to get free shit.

I find a common thing for many newly diagnosed celiacs is to try all things they see labelled gluten free because, well, it's labelled gluten free. Which is super exciting when you thought you would never eat or enjoy food again. Newly diagnosed people spend a lot of time agonizing over all the BROW (barley, rye, oats, wheat)-containing foods they can't have anymore. The horrible thing is that highly processed gluten-free foods generally lack nutrition and are packed with added sugar, salt, and fat to improve the flavours and textures. When you're celiac and you transition to a gluten-free diet, it is typical to gain weight because your intestines start to heal, and you begin absorbing nutrients again. The catch is that you absorb nutrients and everything else too. Add in the excitement of seeing all these foods you believed you would never have again—it's no wonder you buy one of everything and try it all! Here I was bakery hopping, when before I was gluten free, I had zero desire to eat baked goods. Though I love to treat people with a cake on their special day from a fabulous bakery, I generally don't eat sweets.

Although I was super grateful for the freebies and all the incredible options available to me, I felt bad for turning down the free offers.

I couldn't believe the amount of food people wanted to send me to try and give blog reviews on. As someone who once utilized food banks and soup kitchens and would have done just about anything to stay fed, I felt awful for refusing them. What I didn't realize at the time, however, was that there was a connection between what I was creating for the gluten-free community online, the growing gluten-free food industry, and people's willingness to give the gift of food.

By 2017 I had long paid off all my debt and was living comfortably with money in the bank, so I made the choice to leave my corporate job to stay at home with Hubby's dad who suffers from chronic obstructive pulmonary disease. It was a huge transition for me after years of working six days a week, nine to fifteen hours a day (give or take with the commute). I loved my job and all the people I worked with, but I always felt unfulfilled. However, there was one company in particular that I had worked for that sparked something new in me. It was focused on charity and non-profit. It was a side of business I had not seen, and it stuck with me. The idea of helping others and giving back had ignited something in me. I had been building up the blog and lots of exciting things were happening in the gluten-free community. I started wondering how I could transition all my skills and experience from my corporate life and experience with charity work to "the blog."

Being home with Hubby's dad, I had time on my hands that I needed to fill. Work had always been my escape, and now I was left with my thoughts, so I had to get busy. I started reaching out to people in the community and collecting recipes. My brilliant plan was to make a cookbook! I had zero experience and no idea how to do it, but I was determined to create a community cookbook to help people transition to a gluten-free life. One of my main goals was for it to be diverse because it is a misconception that celiac is a "white man's disease"; it doesn't discriminate, and it affects people of all cultures and ages. I wanted it to be an inclusive project and not only be filled with recipes from amazing chefs so that it seemed unattainable to cook like that at home. It needed to be real and relatable to show people that no matter what their skills were in the kitchen, tasty options were awaiting them. I wanted to show people that no matter what you liked to eat, there was a delicious substitute that was safe so you and your whole family could enjoy gluten-free food together. So, I got to work on this project, which was going to keep me busy and learning new skills.

I continued connecting with people in the community, like Ashley from Celiac and the 6ix, and exploring different aspects of wellness, but I felt compelled to do more—simply sharing my day-to-day life was not enough. I wanted to raise awareness for celiac disease as well as help people who needed help with access to safe food while experiencing food insecurity. I reached out to Food Banks Canada among other organizations, and they suggested I connect with Daily Bread, a larger organization that at the time serviced more than 300 food programs across Toronto. In April 2018, I launched an online fundraiser, and my community came together to raise $1,000 for this amazing organization. *A thousand dollars!*

I was amazed by the support from the community and felt inspired to do more. I reached out to RonniLyn Pustil, founder of Gluten-Free Garage, Toronto's pop-up gluten-free market. Gluten-Free Garage is an annual gluten-free food festival that takes place in May during Celiac Awareness Month. Founded in 2012 by RonniLyn after her daughter Lily was diagnosed with celiac at the age of three, GFG showcases seventy-five gluten-free vendors—and the entire event is celiac safe! People come to GFG from all over the province to discover new gluten-free brands, to hear talks, and to see demos and presentations on the gluten-free lifestyle. In 2018 I had the opportunity to sit on a panel of gluten-free "influencers" from across Toronto.

I approached RonniLyn to see if she would allow me to host a gluten-free food drive at the event. We agreed to collaborate! In May 2018, I hosted the first GFREEWIFEY FOOD BANK at Gluten-Free Garage. At the time, I was driving a Honda Fit and announced my goal to "Fill the Fit" with gluten-free non-perishables . . . and did we ever fill it! Thanks to all the amazing attendees at this event, we donated 200 pounds of gluten-free food to the Red Cross Mobile Food Bank.

After this event, the Canadian Celiac Association (CCA) reached out to me directly to support individuals who had been contacting them for support with access to safe food. This connection solidified that I needed to keep doing what I was doing.

The CCA was not the only association to reach out to me after this successful event. People in the community who heard that I was making contributions to organizations reached out, wondering where I brought the food because their food banks were unable to support them or offer safe gluten-free options. I felt bad that I did not have more to give, so I decided to do another fundraiser to help a different local food bank while raising awareness for celiac disease. Food Banks Canada and

Daily Bread connected me with The Stop, which has a larger community that requires access to safe gluten-free food. This time I ran an awareness fundraiser in partnership with The Butternut Baking Co., a gluten-free bakery in Toronto that is also grain free, sugar free, paleo and keto friendly. I loved connecting with each person who came into the bake shop. It felt so fulfilling to be raising awareness about celiac disease and the need for access to safe gluten-free food while ensuring a seamless quality experience that garnered praise from the customers. The Butternut Baking Co. community collectively contributed a $1,000 donation, which we presented to The Stop food bank in August 2018.

That fall, as I was feeling the momentum that we were building for awareness for the cause, I was nominated for the Community Champion award by Daily Bread. I remember being at the award ceremony in a room full of people who were representing large corporations that supported the food bank (think Walmart, Campbell's, provincial associations). What a strange feeling when they announced my name as one of the nominees among these large companies!

In October 2018, I ran my first 5K and raised $1,000 for the CCA to help raise more awareness for the cause. This triggered the CCA to start looking into national gaps in the food-security sector. In January 2019, I accompanied the executive director of the CCA to a meeting with Food Banks Canada, which at the time committed to adding "gluten free" to its data collection upon its new program release in about two years, which would give them the ability to obtain a snapshot of partner food banks that showed how many people required access to gluten-free food at any given time. This kind of data is currently inconsistent and is often not collected.

It is said that 1 percent of the population is affected by celiac disease. That number is increasing, and it is now reported to be closer to 3 percent. Based on all of my work with #GFREEWIFEYFOODBANK, I believe those numbers have been underestimated. The community organizations and non-profits are trying to provide anywhere between 3 and 30 percent of their communities with access to safe gluten-free food.

Shortly after the holidays, I ran an amazing community food drive, partnering with some of the best gluten-free businesses with which I had relationships. I wanted to not only support the food bank clients but also the small businesses that dedicate their lives and businesses to providing food for the gluten-free community. I had the food collection boxes stationed at these shops, and in January 2019, we donated 200 pounds of food to The Mississauga Food Bank.

A new and exciting allergy-friendly vendor fair was launching in Mississauga in March 2019—the Free From and Allergy-Friendly Expo—and I was invited to host a food drive at the entrance. From the shoppers and vendors, we collected 400 pounds of food that was donated to The Mississauga Food Bank. I had to call Hubby near the end of the day to ask him to bring his big truck to come pick me up because there was no way it was going to fit in my car! This was my first "BUY 2, DONATE 1" campaign designed to support the local small businesses and vendors who provide gluten-free foods, while also giving attendees the chance to support neighbours experiencing food insecurity. We had so many incredible brands at the end of the event that contributed to an unsold surplus that I held over for an organization I had just discovered with a population requiring gluten-free food. Overall, another 100 pounds of food went to Feed It Forward after that event.

It had been a year, and what a year it had been. It was already Celiac Awareness Month again! That May 2019, I released the self-published GFREEWIFEY COMMUNITY COOKBOOK. It took me a year to make it and featured sixty-five contributors from across the country who shared their favourite gluten-free recipes. People in the community submitted their recipes. I made the recipes, photographed them, then donated the prepared food to people experiencing food insecurity. The money raised from the sale of the books went back into the food bank projects. We sold 300 copies of that book. I ended that same month hosting my second Gluten-Free Garage food drive. This incredible community of shoppers and vendors came together and blew our first year results out of the park to donate 900 pounds of non-perishables to the Second Harvest and Food Rescue. We agreed it was a great partnership and that the food would stay in the community, and so it was donated to the Wychwood Drop-In. By this point, I had more people and organizations contacting me directly, so I held back some food for people whose food banks did not support them and started a list of registered clients who we provided safe gluten-free food boxes to directly.

The last event I spoke at where I also hosted a food drive was The Gluten-Free Collective in Kitchener–Waterloo. This lively event, run by Sarah Hignell and Elizabeth Siddorn, garnered 155 pounds of food for the Food Bank of Waterloo region.

Holiday 2019 was when I made the commitment to go all in for the people who needed support. The workload was immense—collecting, sorting, and distributing food while trying to educate, inform, and raise awareness. Although it was my passion project, I was just one person who had other obligations. I realized I would have to find a more effective way to educate food banks on safe food handling, storing, and providing access. I was now on the board of directors of the CCA, so getting a national strategy in place could more easily be adopted by a national organization while I focused on the growing list of people through the greater Toronto area I was now hand-delivering food boxes to. Thanks to my amazing partner businesses, we collected and distributed another 200 pounds of food that season. With the switch to direct client support and the growing support of contributors and supporting brands, my living room became a warehouse and Hubby realized the magnitude of my little side project. At a time when I needed to make a decision to either grow or fold the food bank initiative, a global pandemic hit that changed the whole world. That spring, all my in-person speaking engagements and food-drive events were cancelled, and all the partner shops that hosted the drop-off boxes were closed to the public. Food banks saw a surge in users, as many people lost jobs, and the way they served the community became even more restrictive.

During the 2020 pandemic, I ran four virtual campaigns that enabled me to collect and distribute over 2,600 pounds of food and $1,500 to help people trying to survive the pandemic. The CCA released a national sticker program in December to enable donors to educate their local food banks, one sticker at a time. The hope is that when the food bank receives the product with the gluten-free label and storing instructions, it will be saved for someone who requires access to gluten-free food.

I think my story illustrates that one person's drive and determination can make a difference, but it takes a village to make it actually happen. I had an idea and I put it into action to facilitate food drives and fundraisers, but each and every person who donated—whether it was one non-perishable food item, $25, or $1,000—made a difference. That one person who gave me a hand when I was in a tough spot, by handing me a note, affected my life so profoundly that I continue to pay it forward any way I can. That one small act of kindness you do for a person can change the world in ways you may never know. When you are shopping, whether you have food allergies or intolerances or not, I ask you to think about what you would need in a food box if you were having a tough month. Please grab two and donate one.

It's not about knowing what you're doing or if it will work or how to make it work. You just do it and learn along the way, and it is crazy how your passion can create a thing of its own! Now, my passion project that started as a personal blog is on its way to being a registered non-profit. As I navigate the fallout of a pandemic and explore partnership options with various charities and non-profits, I trust that what will be will be and that what we have done together does not stop here. My dream was always to grow my food bank initiative into a holistic project—providing access to safe whole food with urban and vertical farming, providing job opportunities as well as life and workforce training to help people in a tough spot find employment, while growing the food to nourish them forward. Because community is everything and we are all in this together.

From 2017 to 2020, my passion project #GFREEWIFEYFOOD-BANK raised $6,000 and collected 5,000 pounds of gluten-free food to support people experiencing food insecurity on a gluten-free diet. Anything can happen in life; you never know when you might need to grab that helping hand!

Thanks to every individual who contributed to the #GfreeWifeyFoodBank GoFundMe and who brought a gluten-free non-perishable to an event or partner drop-off location. No matter your contribution, know you made a difference. Every dollar counts! Every item fills a hungry tummy! To the gluten-free small business owners for housing the drop-off crates in your shops and for your continued collaboration:

Cal and Isabelle Barron: Cal's Bakery, Barrie

Gabriella Caruso: The Layered Shop, Nobelton

Kenzie Goodall: Sugar Suite Cakes, Oakville

Joan Hepburn: Joanie's Pastries, London

Vicky Matheson: Winnie's Gluten-free, Kitchener

Alannah Wakefield: Nutrition Kitchen, Bowmanville

Joanna Bastas: Buddha Belly Bakery, Newcastle

Suzie Lanktree: Gluten Free by Suzie, Kitchener

Continued thanks to the many corporate donors who send shipments of food to fill the boxes: Ital Pasta, Queen's Street Bakery, Kinnikinnick Foods, Martin's Apples, Fody Foods, Promise Gluten Free, Only Oats, and so many more I simply can't list you all here. Please view the complete list on my website.

Thank you to each of these major contributors: James Hayes and Jeff Onions.

Thank you to my mom, Belinda, and sister, Alexis, for being my lead volunteers.

Thanks, Hubby, for putting up with me converting the living room into a warehouse for months on end and during every food drive I do.

Thank you, vendor fair leaders: RonniLyn Pustil, Sara Hignell and Elizabeth Siddorn, Jackie Fenton, and Eric Dessai for trusting me to be one of the first faces your visitors see as they drop off a donation at your event.

Thanks to you all who go shopping, and please remember to **BUY TWO, DONATE ONE** to help your local community.

To make a contribution, visit
https://www.gofundme.com/f/gfreewifey-foodbank-2021

Jessica Danford is the founder of the popular gluten-free  blog *GFREE-WIFEY*. She also serves on the board of directors for the Canadian Celiac Association. Dedicated to minimizing food insecurity on a gluten-free diet, she founded #GFREEWIFEYFOODBANK in 2018. Jessica advocates for and provides access to safe food by partnering with local businesses and community leaders. As a proven and effective community builder, she brings people together to produce "Community Cookbooks" that empower people to share and live their best gluten-free life. Recently, her platform has evolved to become the "Self-Empowerment Studio," a virtual wellness community that motivates, inspires, and empowers women to love themselves and become who they want to be. Jessica also hosts her new podcast, *Shit That Keeps Me Up at Night*, on which she shoots the shit about the everyday hardships of life, including anxiety, self-doubt, addictions, and mental health struggles. Jessica's life experiences shaped her into a resilient and inspirational role model.

Chapter Nine

Keep Your Own Promise: Pushing through Ageism

Catherine Smith RPN

Should I retire or enrol in college? At sixty, after years upon years of investing in myself, trying new employment avenues, and jumping on newfound opportunities left and right, I found myself at a fork in the road. One way suggested I was perhaps too old to keep pushing forward in the workforce. The other way introduced me to a concept that flagged the "too old" ideology as nonsensical.

I was introduced to the term "ageism" in 2012. While working as an RPN visiting nurse for a home-care agency, I enrolled in my fifth and sixth nursing continuing education courses that year. I had the energy to do online studies, to work, and to take care of home life. The fifth course was health assessment that included clinical demonstration and was an important nursing upgrade. I nailed it with an A+ grade! The sixth course was a study in cultural competence for nurses, providing insight on how to provide culturally competent and inclusive care to all clients, including seniors!

Wait a minute . . . I'm a senior!

Included in the study were stereotypical cartoons and commercials on YouTube to further emphasize the author's point on misconceptions about the older population and illustrate that ageism is a biased attitude. As nurses, we were not to presume lack of cognitive understanding or ability based on a birthdate.

My sixty-year-old eyes stared at the screen.

Was it time to retire? Why was I enrolled in a college credit course? Now I was wondering whether the younger students rolled their eyes over my participation in discussions during those online group studies. Perhaps they learned to apply cultural competence so that I felt included and valued, just like we were being trained to do. My head was swirling with thoughts. At age sixty, it is easy to stop trying. At age sixty in the health care profession, you begin to realize that many of your clients are within your age demographic and that your supervisors, colleagues, and fellow students are millennials. Just like that, everything felt backward. So, let's rewind and take a trip down memory lane where I wasted few opportunities and trusted myself to just try.

1971

One year out of high school, I got married. I worked in office, retail, and hospital settings, helping my young husband gain a college diploma. After he entered his field of employment, I enrolled in nursing. I had experience working as an aide and decided to pursue a registered designation. My first attempt was dismal. I had enrolled in a two-year RN program and quit after six months. I was not prepared for the depth of study, and I lacked confidence. In truth, I lost my nerve. I recall the day I decided to throw in the towel and walk away from my pursuit of higher education.

Things sometimes happen for a reason.

While sitting on the Greyhound bus travelling back along the rural highway, I was startled to see the head nurse of the community hospital where I worked as an aide. I wanted to shrink down in my seat, hoping she wouldn't notice me. I was the quitter! What would she think of me now? We did speak as we departed from the bus. Standing there, I confessed my actions. Her reaction was not what I had expected. She actually agreed with me that the program may have been overwhelming and suggested I consider the next level, the nursing assistant program. She offered to provide me with a reference.

It was a time of reflection. I took her advice and applied to a nursing assistant program offered at a hospital near my parents. I was accepted and would start classes in September 1977. I was excited and proud to have picked myself up and taken on a new challenge after my failed attempt.

It's all about me.

I do recall calling my mother to tell her the great news about enrolling and that I would come and stay with them weekly until the following May! I was the youngest in the family, and I thought she would be thrilled to have my company once again. Her response was a little flat, actually! Both my parents were always loving and supportive, and I was surprised by her reaction.

"What do you want to do that for?" she asked.

My inner voice was thinking, *uh-oh*! It had not occurred to me that my intuitive mother may have read this action of mine as a signal of marriage problems. She would be proven right later on, but I had not yet openly acknowledged that part of my story.

For the first time, I felt I had gained confidence and credible skills.

I could have perceived her response as a block, but I moved forward. I knew I wanted to enter the health care field for myself. So, my mother and I talked, she understood, and my parents welcomed my arrival.

In reflection, I am now the age they were during this time. As a young woman, it never occurred to me that my presence may have affected their daily life while they accommodated me.

Keep going.

I cannot measure the invaluable experience I gained as a student nursing assistant. The effort it took to attend and push through was worth it! For the first time, I felt I had gained confidence and credible skills.

I was voted in as class president, I received the academic award and the nurse proficiency award, and I made new friends. I was maturing!

After graduating, I accepted a nursing position at the local community hospital where I had previously worked. I took on a second part-time job at a long-term care facility as a nurse manager two nights per week. I liked the responsibility!

1979

Starting, stopping, and starting again.

The theme of starting, stopping, and starting again would repeat itself through the years as I ended my first marriage and carved out a life with my second husband (the love of my life) in northern Ontario where I knew no one!

There were few nursing opportunities in the north for registered nursing assistants (RNAs). After four months, I was hired on as casual staff at the local hospital. The closest nursing homes were at least sixty to one hundred kilometres in any direction. The hospital setting did provide me with great experience, and it was nice to get to know other staff.

The role of the RNA was still limited in scope and practice at the time, so any concept of growth opportunities within health care were few. I knew that moving to a rural area in the north would limit my work opportunities, but I also knew I had followed my heart. Well, no harm in changing gears, right?

Do not be afraid to try something else.

While working the odd shift at the hospital, I took the opportunity to accept a position as a store manager in the local mall. It was a paycheque. I will share the following story.

I had helped a customer find just the right pair of jeans in the store one afternoon. She was pleased with her purchase and thanked me for my help. That evening, I worked at the hospital. A patient had arrived at emergency requiring some non-life-threatening attention. I was there to assist. The patient looked at me from the stretcher and asked, "Weren't you the lady who sold me jeans today?" How would this patient view our patient confidentiality? Had I made the right choice?

1982

When you keep yourself open to new ideas, opportunities will show up.
Our town had received funding for a social services program. A program coordinator was sought to manage and develop a training program for clients on social assistance. I applied with the confidence that my nursing skills could be used in helping those candidates who found themselves on social assistance. I was hired.

Pay attention to what your inner voice is telling you.
I developed a three-month work-related training module. I quickly recognized that the candidates were quite ready to dive in, and they enabled the success of the program. I seemed to automatically create a team spirit within the training program without micromanaging the candidates. They were adults with multiple skills.

The candidates produced a weekly newsletter providing a meaningful employment experience. Years down the road, I would draw on this experience.

Satellite TV had just arrived in our town, and I made a futile attempt to develop my own home-grown business, after my time with the program. I purchased my first home computer in order to produce a simple TV guide. Updates from broadcasters came in the mail, and I worked in DOS format. Although I did sway a few businesses to pay for ads, my little entity flopped. Perhaps working alone was not my comfort level.

The municipal office did invite me back to briefly work as a consultant to help with the application process for a new funding incentive. Why not?

Be open to new learning opportunities.

In 1982 I also enrolled in my first continuing education course for RNAs in areas of diabetes and medications. I respected the need to remain relevant and competent in nursing, even though I worked very few hours at the hospital. This decision proved to play an important step later on. Course instruction took place at the high school, years before online learning would present new opportunities. After completing the upgrade course, I accepted a position as nurse/reception for a local chiropractic clinic. I applied nursing skills to prepare clients for procedures, including X-rays and hot and cold therapy applications, while managing the office and appointments.

My résumé was now looking more solid from a health care perspective.

1984

I was three months into the job, and two months into my first pregnancy. I recall my manager calling me at home one evening. I had made a mistake in processing a report for his physician's fees, and he was not pleased. I really felt quite bad. I owned the error! I did let him know that I would not continue at the office. I had developed a concern about the proximity of the X-ray equipment in the workspace due to my pregnancy. I advised him that I knew someone who would be suitable for the position and that I would contact her. He welcomed the suggestion. It was the right thing to do.

Opportunity knocks again!

At this point, should I have been checking the local papers for job ads?

The local insurance office was advertising for a clerk. I attended an interview, and apparently, they liked the idea that my father had been a career insurance salesman, and I had a very prudent belief in all things insurance. I started the next week. After a couple of weeks at work, the owners asked me if I would be interested in selling general insurance for them, as they had observed how easily I engaged with their clients. The only catch was that I would need to acquire my insurance broker's licence, and that meant attending a course in Toronto. Could I go in January?

Starting, stopping, and starting again.

Here I go again! I probably should have said no thank you, but I accepted this new challenge. I flew down to Toronto, stayed with family, and took the two-week broker course. I was six months pregnant, and I was the only attendee in the class who had permission to take a bathroom break whenever needed. I successfully passed the course, but I do recall the exhaustion once back home.

Our first daughter was born April 29, 1985. She changed our lives forever. As new parents, my husband and I were both thrilled and terrified. Family came to visit and helped through those first weeks. I did find myself becoming exhausted and needing more sleep than I was permitted.

Ageism creeps in at different stages of your life.

I appreciated the early spring weather and often took our baby daughter out in the carriage, walking around the neighbourhood in our community. Why did I feel self-conscious? Why did I feel "older?" I did notice that I was a decade older than most of the other young moms I knew. It was a fleeting thought. It was not so much that I felt older, rather that I felt inexperienced, and I did not have the day-to-day extended family support that others enjoyed. In reflection, I think I felt somewhat lonely.

I returned to work after four months. I had connected with a lovely lady in town with three school-aged daughters, who was more than happy to provide our daughter with very nurturing care as I returned to the office.

Never burn bridges.

I had separation anxiety on some days when I took our baby to the sitter's and headed to work. I remember one day in particular when I was working alone at the service counter of the office. I could see through the large front window, and I saw my sitter walking along the sidewalk with my daughter in a stroller sporting a cute sun hat. I stood there staring, tears flowing, questioning myself. Why was I working while our little daughter was enjoying the day without me?

I couldn't wait for the workday to end so I could pick her up and go home.

Where was the time going?

1989

We purchased two hundred acres about five kilometres outside of our little town and built our home. Our daughter had started junior kindergarten half days, and we relied on school buses. Formal daycare was not available, and we needed to find a new sitter. We were not about to leave our daughter with just anyone.

I would stay home.

I struggled between the emotional need of staying home and the desire of working outside the home. I belonged to the generation that stayed home with children, but I also observed parents ten years younger than I who were juggling work and childcare. At age thirty-seven, I was between two mindsets.

1990

It is never too late.

I now required a flexible work schedule. My present job required a five-day work week. The concept of a home office had not yet arrived, nor had the internet for home use.

I had two provincial licences, one for insurance and one for nursing.

I called the College of Nurses. I met their requirement for returning to nursing practice within their five-year limit, as I had also completed a course upgrade. I was granted a licence to practice nursing.

A new community hospital had just been built. The addition of a long-term care wing provided new opportunities for RNAs. I was hired in April 1990. It took a lot of nerve to walk through the hospital doors and report to the head nurse. I had to become familiar with new surroundings and a new routine. I was provided with

I was provided with opportunities to refresh and test my skills, and before long, I gained confidence.

opportunities to refresh and test my skills, and before long, I gained confidence.

My work schedule allowed the flexibility I was seeking, and a short year later I knew I was pregnant. It was a wonderful time.

1992

Never give up.

I don't ever recall during any of those years feeling too old to start something new. I never really felt the need to compete or feel jealous of someone younger until February 19, 1992, when I lost our infant son after a twenty-week pregnancy. He came too early, and he couldn't survive. I was thirty-nine and devastated.

I had to be transported by helicopter to Sudbury. I remember lying on the stretcher thinking if I didn't move or breathe too hard, then I would be able to hold onto our baby. I focused on the watch I was wearing. I watched the minute hand moving time.

But it was not to be. My husband and I were both deeply saddened. We thought perhaps we would try again. The grief came in waves. Family and friends tried to provide emotional support for me and gently suggested that perhaps it was too late for me to have another baby.

I needed to take time from work. I found that I would sum up the courage to accept a shift and be excited to go, only to break down and cancel. Too soon. But remember, I had a little daughter at home, and she unknowingly helped me through that dark time. She was seven years old and full of life, and I knew I could not let my sadness affect her. After all, she was now a Brownie, and we needed to sell cookies door to door! I felt like I was walking through quicksand. I pushed through.

Ageism creeps in at different stages of your life.

My husband, daughter, and I attended a friend's home for an afternoon party. I didn't realize the party was for my fortieth birthday! I received birthday cards with the typical "over forty" jokes, and I buried the hurt. No one knew how I felt, of course, or knew of our plans to have another baby before it was biologically too late. One younger mother had brought her infant daughter to the party. I used my humour to push through and then quietly broke down after returning home.

1993

At age forty-one, I brought my second daughter into the world on November 18, 1993. It took a two-month stay in hospital in order to bring her to term. She had to remain in ICU for the first two days. I recall clearly my need to be with her, so I got out of bed, still very sore from the abdominal incision, and slowly walked down the hallway using the handrail for support. I had to see her, to make sure she was alright. She was perfect.

My husband returned the next day with our daughter, and we sat by her infant sister for the first time as a family.

Losing focus.

A year later, I found myself in a mild depression. Feelings of isolation crept in. I seemed to yearn for something beyond our little town. I had planned to visit my mother-in-law in Toronto with our two girls for a week before Halloween and ended up staying for almost a month. My marriage had become strained by this time. Looking back, I think the time away was necessary for me. Our oldest daughter was now in grade four, and I made arrangements for her to attend the neighbourhood school during our stay. She appeared to like meeting new friends, especially a little girl from Russia. I expected her to readjust after we returned home. She did. Kids can be resilient, but I still question my judgment.

1996

Staying relevant.

Work, it seemed, provided me with a sense of belonging and engagement, which was how I managed my feelings of isolation.

In 1996 I enrolled in a course for the study of aseptic procedures. The location of the course was eighty kilometres away. This commute was hard to juggle with a three-year-old and an eleven-year-old at home. My husband provided huge support while juggling his own career.

1997

Starting, stopping, and starting again.

In 1975 I had had a knee injury requiring surgery. That injury caught up with me in 1997. Surgery exposed a deteriorated knee joint with some range of motion limitation. I left hospital work and felt the frustration.

After contemplating returning to office work, I was advised that I could regain my broker's licence if a brokerage sponsored me. I established a commissioned-based relationship with a brokerage in Sudbury and worked out of my own office in town. This step put me in the right position to accept an offer by the local insurance office to return as manager, as the owners were retiring.

In reflection, I seemed to adapt from one vocation to the other quite smoothly.

The skill set could not have been more different, but the common thread of customer/client service was really what I was tapping into, as helping people solve problems was my thing.

2003

Summing up the nerve.

I turned fifty-one. In 2003 home care opened up for RPNs in our area. Private agencies were now acquiring government contracts, hiring RPNs and personal support workers, and that changed everything. I knew I could physically manage home visits as opposed to twelve-hour hospital shifts.

Did I have the nerve at age fifty-one? Would human resources take me seriously? Could I learn new skills? Our daughters were now ten and eighteen, and our eldest was on her way to university.

Ageism creeps in at different stages of your life.

The first action I took was the easiest. I contacted the College of Nurses once again and arranged for validating my registration. The next action was attending a job interview. I felt nervous walking into that agency that day and "pretending" I was a nurse! Would they perceive me as being old and outdated and view me through the eyes of ageism?

The HR manager kindly viewed me as a competent candidate, and although she knew I had been away from nursing practice, she said, "No worries. Nursing is just like riding a bicycle; you never forget."

She was quite right, and I never forgot the opportunity she provided me. Home care was my thing! It required a nurse to work autonomously as well as to have the maturity, skills, and an empathetic attitude to visit clients in their homes.

From 2003 to 2013, I was enrolled in either a workshop or online college upgrade courses. For the first time, my role included training personal support workers (PSWs). These workers could be assigned or delegated certain procedures or tasks for a specific client who is considered medically stable. Experience gained in training and mentoring for the next thirteen years provided me with the foundation for what was to come next.

Starting, stopping, and starting again.

I reached a point when travelling to do home-care visits seemed tiring. Was it burnout, or was it the fact that I was now sixty-five? How could I apply my experience with mentoring and training PSWs beyond home-care visits?

2017

Ageism creeps in at different stages of your life.

An employment ad in the local paper caught my attention. Here I go again, right? The area college was looking for nurse instructors for the personal support worker program that would begin in September. I applied by email and attached my long résumé. I did not receive a response. What was I thinking? The College would want someone young and dynamic. I dismissed the idea and, at the same time, cut back on my work.

Opportunity knocks again!

The College did contact me later that fall and offered me the winter term contract, starting in January. The privilege of providing classroom instruction for the personal support worker program was humbling. The students were halfway to their goal of graduating. Home care was put on hold. I developed course outlines, lesson plans, and created PowerPoint presentations. The idea of ageism vanished, replaced by my enthusiasm.

2018

Courage!

Twelve young women arrived on day one. I quickly learned that they had been comfortable with their previous instructor, and they expressed feelings of disappointment about the change. It did not occur to me until that morning that the students would feel this way. It became very clear that I was more excited about my presence than they were, and I understood. Those twelve women taught me more about their world as adult students juggling numerous issues and responsibilities while trying to obtain a college certificate than I taught them about anatomy!

They helped me make use of a Google drive so that I could share lesson plans and assignments within a virtual space. Nurses do not necessarily make good instructors. Not all adults learn the same way. I listened to their life stories.

The term ended, and I believe most felt successful in their accomplishment and moved on to apply their skills in the health care sector.

Reflecting on the experience, I wished I had been a more effective instructor.

2019

Taking action.

I enrolled in a year-long online college certificate program in Adult Education for Teaching and Instruction. I learned how to motivate and engage students and why universal design in learning matters. The online platform was essential for my participation.

I was offered another opportunity to instruct a three-week workshop for PSW employees in March 2019. I was able to apply new concepts. I developed the lesson plans based on the identified skills gap and delivered the workshops to some very engaging PSWs from whom I also learned ways of traditional care within their Indigenous culture.

2020

I had embraced learning, regardless of my age.

The pandemic hit in mid-March. All workshops and class instruction were cancelled. The health care sector was in crisis, and frontline workers were at the epicentre. I found myself feeling guilty for not seeking reassignment, as there was a literal call to arms for nurses not currently working. At sixty-eight years of age, I knew I could still be of service.

The College contacted me to assist in developing an online program for a new Personal Care Aide course. If I had not completed the adult education certificate course, I would not have had the skill set needed for online learning platforms.

I prepared a draft course outline and met with the nursing department chair by phone, and we discussed the *why*, the *what*, and the *how* the course could be relevant to the current community need.

I do not know if my participation in a new course will come to fruition. I am okay with that.

My message is simple. Ageism is a perceived bias. Keep believing in your own ability and challenge yourself to try something new.

I extend my gratitude to the twelve college students and ten workshop PSW attendees who, without knowing, actually empowered me to learn more.

I wish to thank **www.cambriancollege.ca** for providing the opportunity to teach and also **www.georgebrown.ca** for creating meaningful online adult learning platforms.

Regardless of your age or circumstance, never believe you are past the age of trying.

Catherine Smith is a registered practical nurse (RPN) with the College of Nurses in Ontario, a position she's held for forty-one years. She's often taken advantage of opportunities to work in other sectors, mostly out of necessity after moving to northern Ontario. Was she moving away from a  predictable vocation in nursing or was she moving toward a better understanding of what was possible? A pathway to where? Catherine thought many times, "What's the point? Nobody cares if I do this." But she cared, and she found the courage to push through and keep her own promise.

Her goals in life are to experience new challenges for personal and professional growth, to keep family life in balance, and to remain relevant in the senior years. She embraces the concept of lifelong learning.

In 2018 a work experience opened a new pathway, but ageism and fear crept in. She was sixty-seven. At her mature age with no specific work assigned, it was not easy to keep going. Her purpose was clear. She wanted to instruct classes and workshops for adult education within the health care sector. She had taken many college-level nursing courses, but this direction was new for her.

Married for thirty-six years to the love of her life, Catherine and her husband enjoy trips to visit their two daughters and son-in-law, wherever they happen to be living in Canada! In her free time, Catherine enjoys going for walks, being in the great outdoors, and living a healthy senior lifestyle.

Chapter Ten

Trust Yourself Above All Else

Sarah Swain

Oh, my god, my heart is racing. I think I'm going to pass out. Where's the exit?! Shit. There are too many people behind me. I'll never be able to run out of here fast enough. How can I get out of this now?! I can't do this. I'm so underqualified. Who do I even think I am? I'm panicking. BREATHE, Sarah. Focus.

"Everyone please welcome Sarah Smith to the stage."

Shit. It's too late. Get it together, Sarah. Breathe. Just start walking to the stage. One foot in front of the other. It's cool. It's cool. They won't notice your heart beating out of your jugular. Remember to smile. Goddammit! Why did I think four-inch stilettos were a good idea today? Don't fall. Don't fall. Don't fall.

Applause

"Thank you, everyone! Another round of applause for our CEO, Calvin!" I manage to bellow into the mic with the remaining 1.5 cubic centimetres of air left in my barely breathing lungs.

Good move. Distract them and give yourself a moment to catch your breath.
Breathe. You've got this.

Inhale.

"Thank you, everyone! My name is Sarah, and I am thrilled to be here in partnership with corporate headquarters to announce our new retail pricing strategy!"

Exhale.

There you go. You're fine now. Finish off your speech and get off the stage like the mothereffing boss that you are.

I was twenty-four years old, managing a team of 440 people at the flagship Sears location at the Toronto Eaton's Centre. My manager had been promoted to a regional position, and my overly confident and ignorant ass said yes when the regional team asked me to take on the role of acting store manager. I mean, how hard could it be?

Leap. Figure it out on the way down. My life's motto.

✳ ✳ ✳

My parents instilled a high level of confidence within me and built stability around me as I grew up. I can't ever remember a time when I hesitated over taking a chance on myself as a kid. Maybe it was because my mom would put change in my hand as a toddler and encourage me to place my own order for a Happy Meal at McDonalds. Maybe it was because my dad would take me into the woods and teach me how to navigate my way home using a compass and tree markers. Maybe it was the resilience I built from talking myself through the last few breaths before public speaking engagements or the moments leading up to the sound of the starter pistol at track and field meets during elementary school. Perhaps it was all these things that taught me that fear is simply an inevitable part of the process. I was conditioned from a young age to know that fear isn't something that can ever be avoided if you want to achieve something great. The pounding in my chest, the shortness of breath, and the sweating palms became normal physiological side effects to my everyday life as I constantly propelled myself to push my own limits and challenge the depths of my natural aptitudes.

And it all came to a crashing halt in high school. I wasn't one of the lucky ones to come out of those treacherous teenage years unscathed. My nervous system still clenches the way it did at sixteen when I think about it, even though as I write these words, high school was over half my life ago. The soul never forgets. I was fifteen when I started partying, and one night in particular left me in the precarious position of not knowing up from down. My girlfriends and I were drinking with the older boys, some of whom were in their early twenties. At the time, I thought it was cool. Now, just the thought makes my skin crawl. I had a little too much whisky and moonshine (yeah, whisky and moonshine—not sugary fruit coolers or spritzers) and found out the next morning that

I had defecated myself. Yup. I not only shit my pants, but I apparently ripped off my underwear and left them in the bush for the boys to find, marking the beginning of the complete and total destruction of all the confidence I had been raised to know.

The high school hallways became my worst nightmare for the next two years. I could not even escape to my locker to hide my head, as someone had scratched the word "poop" into its metal door, making it impossible for me to erase. My final years of high school, where I should have been out having fun and feeling excited about my future, left me with a sky-high absenteeism record, dropping grades, and a burning desire to escape. I can't even imagine what would've happened if social media existed back then, and my heart agonizes for kids this day and age who experience this level of inexorable mortification. At least back then, my home was my safe space, and Wi-Fi couldn't allow the ridicule and relentless bullying to walk right through my front door and haunt me from a glowing screen beneath my bedsheets for all hours of the night. I don't know whether I would've survived that depth of pain, unable to hide from its source. I couldn't even wait to get off the stage at my own graduation for fear that someone would make a "tooting" sound from the audience, their go-to weapon in the hallways, and effectively put the final nail into the coffin of my high school experience. I went from top-of-the-class honour-roll student and athlete who was a force to be reckoned with to barely scraping by academically, ditching challenging math and science classes that would have granted entry into the top Canadian universities because I just couldn't keep my focus long enough on my studies to pull through. My self-esteem as a young woman had been crushed beneath the weight of the high school success scale that was dangerously tipped toward social status and acceptance. Needless to say, I was out of my tiny hometown the moment I could be, praying that every ounce of pain, shame, and embarrassment would stay in my rearview mirror on the way down the highway.

Fuck this place. Stupid small towns.

My lack of focus in my latter high school years wreaked havoc on me while I bounced around from university to university and major to major in a desperate attempt to find my career calling. I went from a major in business management with a minor in marketing to a major in journalism with a minor in political science to ultimately graduating from college with a diploma in police foundations and law enforcement. Like, what? If I had a flag to wave between the ages of eighteen and twenty-one, it would have said, *"Send a therapist. And a pack of smokes. Du Maurier King Regular, please. I'm fine, I swear."* Truthfully, none of it ended up mattering anyway, as I was far more interested in gaining experience in the workforce, networking and earning money, so much so that I dropped down to part-time studies in my final year of college so I could work full time instead, prolonging my graduation by another semester, which, as you can probably guess, I didn't even attend. *"Send me my diploma in the mail, please. Thanks."*

The workforce challenged me in the ways I used to love feeling challenged as a kid. I felt safe in new places outside of educational institutions that held so many wounds. People often asked me how I was able to just move to the city of Toronto by myself and start figuring things out, but to me, it felt easy and obvious. Not knowing anyone felt like a gift. A breath of fresh air. Safety. A chance to start over again with an untarnished reputation. Just the ability to go to the grocery store without having to check every aisle for assholes first felt like a luxury. The confidence that had been buried somewhere in the depth of my cells was finally starting to return, only I was emerging as someone new, someone more resilient—almost as if I were making up for lost time.

✷ ✷ ✷

Sarah, will you be an undercover shopper and arrest shoplifters?

Yes.

Sarah, will you conduct internal theft and fraud investigations?

Yes.

Sarah, will you take on a supervisory role?

Yes.

Sarah, will you take on a bigger team?

Yes.

Sarah, will you take on a management role?

Yes.

Sarah, will you take on a district position?

Yes.

Sarah, will you take a role in Operations?

Yes.

Sarah, will you run our flagship location?

Yes.

Sarah, will you make a speech on stage with the CEO?

Yes . . .

I remember not being able to understand the gut-churning amount of fear I felt in the moments walking onto the stage. I had said yes to, tackled, and aced just about every professional opportunity earned up until that point in my tiny career at age twenty-four. Why this? Why was this the thing that was challenging me the most? It wasn't until several years later that I began to understand the deeply rooted fear I had developed of being seen in spaces where I couldn't control my surroundings or my exits. After all, I had spent my emerging adult years lying low and carefully planning my routes and social outings to save myself from harassment, despite my confident exterior façade. It was my first time stepping on a stage again, and despite my childhood public speaking competition experience, I suddenly felt terrified as a young adult. Yet as much as my insides were screaming and toiling into cramps, and my brain was screaming for me to run out the door and into the nearest subway station, my legs propelled me forward. Why? How? What I know now that I didn't know then is that my Soul knew the pain of turning around, and running would have far exceeded the pain of face-planting on the stage in front of nearly 2,000 of my colleagues and superiors. My intuition knew, and it overrode my ego without me even being aware of it. That's some incredible, innate human magic. The pain of regret is far more excruciating than the pain of failure. Neither are easy. One is just easier. And somewhere deep inside me, stuffed down beneath all the fear and layers of patchy cement armour I had built up around my dignity, something was strong enough to shine through the cracks and take the lead.

Getting my physical body up and onto that stage and speaking into the mic with the CEO standing beside me while my heart pounded out of my chest was a pivotal moment in my career. I think I was on stage for all of seven minutes, but those seven minutes reminded me of the gifts on the other side of the nerves that I had learned as a child. It was all coming back.

My career for the next several years took me down all kinds of wild paths of various opportunities, mixed with a move across the country with my now-husband, who at the time I had only been dating for about a year. I stayed within the world of retail operations and ran flagship retail stores in Edmonton, where the hunger for driving sales really sunk into my cells. Often the youngest of my peers, I was usually seen as the *rogue millennial* who took on this seemingly *bizarre* approach to leadership that focused heavily on fun, innovation, personal development, and friendly competitions for my teams. I can recall one particular contest that I hosted for my employees. They were to collect customer service surveys, and the winner got to be the store manager for the day while I worked in their role for their scheduled shift. The winner of the competition was scheduled as a cashier on the winning day, so I rang in customer sales all day while she proudly took over the store, manager clipboard in hand. Leading people was becoming a passion that allowed me to see just how capable and driven people could be once I figured out what made them tick. I was hooked, and the little flame inside that had dulled to a tiny ember was roaring again.

By my late twenties, I was beginning to see a pattern in my career that looked a whole lot like a hamster wheel. The moment I started to feel unchallenged, I would become bored, that boredom would turn into stagnancy, and I'd soon be looking for the next opportunity. Repeat. Repeat. Repeat. My mom used to joke with me on our long-distance phone calls, "It's been three months, dear, what new work adventure are you onto now?" My skill set was vast because of my willingness to jump into new opportunities or take on new projects, so I always felt like I had options that I was equally proud of and grateful for. I paid attention to the initiatives the companies I was working for seemed to value the most. I would then double down on my efforts in those areas, which not only drove my results but also led me to a constant stream of learning opportunities and experiences, many of which I have taken with me into my own businesses today.

When I had some time off work, I would often make my way back to northern Ontario to visit my parents. Flights, rental cars, and lots of planning would make it possible, even though it was cheaper for me to fly to Mexico for a seven-day, all-inclusive trip—gotta love domestic Canadian airline travel! My parents lived pretty rural, which made me feel a little safer each time I returned to the place that left me so torn up inside. I would carefully turn off the highway and onto the dirt road that led me home without showing my face in town. Even a whole decade later, my body would get tighter and tighter the closer I got to my little town, a town that didn't deserve for me to hate it as much as I did. Leaving helped me for a couple of reasons, though. It helped me grow to appreciate my roots again. I noticed I had a lot of skills and childhood experiences that many of my new friends didn't have. I knew how to bait my own hooks and fish. I knew how to drive snowmobiles, boats, and ATVs. I knew how to safely and responsibly operate firearms. I knew how to use a compass and make campfires. I knew different species of trees, fish, and birds, and I could identify animals and their likely proximity based on their droppings and how long they'd been there (*thanks, Dad*). I actually wasn't afraid of bears until I moved to the city where a strong narrative of the danger of bears and other wildlife existed, instead of people being equipped to know how to be safe out in the wild. Didn't everyone have a bear named Billy and hawk named Buddy that hung around their property? I suppose not. So, each time I'd arrive at *The Ranch* over time, I'd find it easier to collapse into a state of total relaxation and appreciation for where I came from, and my feelings of resentment were suddenly replaced with guilt for loathing something so great, so deeply. Leaving is what I had to do, though. Even if it was done in such haste. For my fragile teenage-girl ego that felt like my world was finished before I even got a chance to begin, it was paramount I consciously and intentionally placed myself into a space that stimulated my self-esteem bit by bit, day by day. Much like a plant, I needed the right environment to grow, flourish, and strengthen. While I feel as though I missed so many years of appreciating my roots, I'm thankful I trusted myself to go out on my own to rediscover my strengths and reconnect to my confident and ambitious inner child that never doubted what she was capable of.

... I'm thankful I trusted myself to go out on my own to rediscover my inner strengths ...

As I forged onward in my professional path, I was fortunate to experience a plethora of career roles that each played small parts in bringing me back to life and reminding me of what I was capable of doing. I grew my leadership skills leading stores, districts, regions, and even all western Canada at one point. I grew my resilience, learning a lot of lessons the hard way and often simply solving problems all week long and not accomplishing much else. One particular experience I had as a Senior Change Agent for a company-wide policy and workflow change I had worked on directly with third-party consultants taught me just how creative I needed to be as a leader in order to lead change. We were told by the consultants to expect a 30 percent turnover in management as we rolled out the change, and they were right. I revitalized my public speaking skills, facilitating countless training sessions in rooms of hundreds of employees from all levels of the organization. I strengthened my communication and conflict resolution skills in heated boardroom discussions and debates. I empowered my voice to speak up when something felt as if it lacked integrity. I learned how to manage my time in dealing with competing priorities and deadlines while juggling flight schedules, meetings, and conference calls. Every single one of these skills can transfer into what I do today as the founder of GCW Publishing House and in the work I do with my own clients to help them build businesses they love. Gratitude doesn't seem like enough some days. I most definitely experienced periods of frustration, irritation, fatigue, self-doubt, and a whole load of other emotions along the way (*and still do!*) that often tempted me to fall back into the false notion of my comfort zone and out of the spotlight, but I'm glad I never let that wounded and scared version of myself take the wheel any longer than I had let her already.

I often wonder what path I would be on now if I had not worked relentlessly to rebuild my confidence again as a young woman. Would I be married to my husband? Would I live in Alberta? Would I have two businesses of my own? Would I know even half the people I do now? The choices we make when we're at are lowest are often the most important choices of all. When we think we don't have any strength left, can we do one more rep? When we think we're out of options, can we find one more thing we haven't tried? When we doubt what we're doing, can we find one more reason to believe? When we feel overcome by fear, can we step into trust? When we feel like we have lost ourselves, can we trust the path forward to rediscover who we are? When a mountain is in our way, can we move it?

Yes. We can.

I'm dedicating this one to me and the little voice that kept whispering to me from within to keep going, and to *The Ranch* for being my safe haven.

Sarah Swain left her six-figure corporate gig in January 2018 with no back-up plan other than *"I trust myself enough to make this happen."* She is now the proud owner of a Canadian Media Company & Publishing House, GCW Publishing, a mentor to emerging leaders in entrepreneurship,  and a strategist to online, service-based business owners. Sarah lives in Alberta, Canada, with her husband, Rob, and when she isn't taking the world of online entrepreneurship by storm, you'll likely to find her soaking up the magic of the Rocky Mountains.

OUTRO

There you have it! Ten women who moved mountains by overcoming personal experiences and professional obstacles as they continued to forge ahead, brilliantly illustrating that there is no one single defined way of leading a professional life. Let these stories serve as a reminder that it's never too late to change your trajectory and the only right way of doing it is the way in which it works for you. Whether your goal is an entirely different career, less or more of what you're currently doing, a leap into entrepreneurship, or constructing a not-for-profit organization, you get to let yourself experience it. You get to lead a fulfilling life, and the best part of that is that the people around you, the ones you love the most, end up benefiting too.

Whoever said you can either live to work or work to live planted a seed in all of us. Being excited to do what you do and feeling proud for how you do it is a gift we want you to give yourself. While the journey won't always be easy, it will always be worth it every step of the way, and when some days feel tougher than others, remember that the work you're doing is far greater than you're likely giving yourself credit for as you move mountains out of the path for those coming up behind you. With each problem you solve, you make it a little easier for someone else. With each new thing you try, you remove more of the stigma attached to doing things differently.

Trust yourself, always.

You'll move mountains, my dear.

For more books by GCW Publishing House, visit gcwpublishing.com.

Reflect & Apply

Was there a particular author with whom you felt you related?

What was it about this author's experience that you felt connected to?

Are you currently navigating a similar situation? In what ways?

Did you find anything within the author's story you feel you can take away to help you navigate your current experience?

What is your desired outcome?

What can you implement in your routine to help you continue to navigate your current experience so that it leads to a desired outcome for you?

Thank you for reading this book and supporting our authors. If you'd like to connect with us or our authors, please be sure to email us at team@thegreatcanadianwoman.ca!

Endnotes

Yulia Eskin

1. The Chernobyl disaster was a nuclear accident that occurred on Saturday, April 26, 1986, in Ukrainian SSR in the Soviet Union and is considered the worst nuclear disaster in history both in terms of cost and casualties. The USSR attempted to conceal the accident from the population. https://en.wikipedia.org/wiki/Chernobyl_disaster

2. The migration policies of the USSR included a virtual abolition of emigration and immigration, an effective ban on private travel abroad, and pervasive controls on internal migration. Beginning in 1987, a year after my birth, Jews were permitted to emigrate. A mass exodus to the USA, Israel, and later Germany, took place. https://www.cambridge.org/core/journals/law-and-social-inquiry/article/abs/what-does-it-mean-to-control-migration-soviet-mobility-policies-in-comparative-perspective/D6938565160FD6D9BCA8822F2C5EA4B7, https://library.fes.de/libalt/journals/swetsfulltext/15286778.pdf

3. The Holocaust was the genocide of European Jews during World War II. Between 1941 and 1945, Nazi Germany and its collaborators systematically murdered some six million Jews across German-occupied Europe, around two-thirds of Europe's Jewish population. Belorussian, Lithuanian, Ukrainian, and Latvian volunteers assisted the Nazi regime with killing sprees in Jewish ghettos in Belarus. https://en.wikipedia.org/wiki/The_Holocaust, https://en.wikipedia.org/wiki/The_Holocaust_in_Byelorussia

4. The USSR official ideology was the elimination of existing religion and the prevention of future implanting of religious belief with the goal of establishing state atheism. The Communist Party destroyed churches, mosques, and synagogues and executed religious leaders. https://en.wikipedia.org/wiki/Religion_in_the_Soviet_Union

5. The Alhambra Decree was an edict issued in 1492 ordering the expulsion of practicing Jews from Spain. As a result, over 200,000 Jews converted to Catholicism and between 40,000 and 100,000 were expelled. The expulsion led to mass migration of Jews from Spain to Italy, Greece, and the Mediterranean Basin. From the thirteenth to the sixteenth centuries, European countries expelled the Jews from their territories on at least fifteen occasions. https://en.wikipedia.org/wiki/Alhambra_Decree, https://en.wikipedia.org/wiki/Expulsion_of_Jews_from_Spain

6. It is heard in a BBC recording from April 20, 1945, of Jewish survivors of the Bergen-Belsen concentration camp five days after their liberation. This was the first Sabbath ceremony openly conducted on German soil since the beginning of the war. With people still dying around them, the survivors sang what would become the Israeli national anthem, "Hatikvah." At the end of "Hatikvah," British Army Chaplain Leslie Hardman shouts out, "Am Yisrael Chai!" https://en.wikipedia.org/wiki/Chai_(symbol)

7. Brown, Brené. *Dare to Lead: Brave Work. Tough Conversations. Whole Hearts.* Random House, 2018.

8. Only 38% of women who majored in computer science are working in the field compared to 53% of men, according to data from the National Science Foundation. This is a consistent trend that has been dubbed a "leaky pipeline," where it's difficult to retain women in STEM jobs once they've graduated with a STEM degree. https://www.cio.com/article/3516012/women-in-tech-statistics-the-hard-truths-of-an-uphill-battle.html#:~:text=The%20retention%20gap&text=Only%2038%25%20of%20women%20who,compared%20to%2030%25%20of%20men.

Stephanie Moram

1. https://richardbrooke.com, retrieved May 27, 2021.

Amanda Lytle

Rotary Youth Exchange is a Rotary International student exchange program for students in secondary school. https://www.rotary.org/en/our-programs/youth-exchanges

Jane Middlehurst

Tara Brach. "Unfolding the Wings of Acceptance." Unfolding the Wings of Acceptance - Tara Brach, retrieved May 25, 2021.

Brown, Brené. *The Gifts of Imperfection: Let Go of Who You Think You're Supposed to Be and Embrace Who You Are.* Hazelden, 2010.

We aren't your average publisher! GCW Publishing House and Media Group™ is a Canadian woman-owned and operated publishing house where we ignite courage and confidence in women worldwide and help them write high-impact, non-fiction books that make waves, move mountains, blaze trails, and change lives! We combine the art of story-telling, connection, camaraderie, support, marketing, and public relations into the book-writing experience to provide our authors with the entire publishing process and beyond!

For more information on publishing, blogging, and podcasting opportunities, please visit: gcwpublishing.com

THE GREAT CANADIAN WOMAN— SHE IS STRONG AND FREE SERIES

An inspiring three-volume series of real-life stories from Canadian women who have overcome life adversities, found a way through seemingly impossible circumstances, and rose above their pain and tribulations. Their courageous stories will instil a sense of hope and empowerment in others so that they, too, can overcome their personal hardships and know they are not alone. These stories grant us all the permission to live fully, love deeply, and fight like hell in the name of happiness.

THE GREAT CANADIAN WOMAN— SHE IS STRONG AND FREE I

The Great Canadian Woman is all of us. She is the single mother who provides for her children come hell or high water. She is the woman who has a dream and musters up enough courage to go after it. She is the woman who has quarreled in the depths of pain and grief and finds her way back home to herself. She is the woman who says no to what does not serve her. She is the woman who says enough is enough and commits to a new way of living. She is the woman who finds the strength to leave toxic relationships. She is the woman who knows unconditional love. She is the woman who takes the lead and lights the torch. She is the woman who refuses to accept the limits that someone else placed before her. She is the woman who knocks down doors and shatters glass ceilings. She is the woman who finds a way out of no way then turns around, extends her hand, and brings as many people as she can along with her. These stories grant us all the permission to live fully, love deeply, and fight like hell in the name of happiness.

THE GREAT CANADIAN WOMAN— SHE IS STRONG AND FREE II

The Great Canadian Woman is every woman. She is overcoming trauma. She is coming to terms with her intuition. She is changing careers and finding a new path. She is grieving while raising her children. She is overcoming racial injustices. She is removing mental health stigmas. She is finding her joy. She is raw and real. She is a light in the darkness. She stumbles and falls, but she rises by sharing her story and speaking her truth. Sometimes we need to break so we can rebuild. In the chapters of this book, these great Canadian women show you how to do just that, through their intense vulnerability, massive strength, immense courage, and endless perseverance.

THE GREAT CANADIAN WOMAN—
SHE IS STRONG AND FREE III

What if we told you that you are not alone in your pain, struggles, or downfalls? That there are women out there who are just like you? Who have been through what you have been through? Who have felt what you have felt? Women who could sit across from you, look you in the eyes, and see you and know what you have been through. Those women exist in this book. They are women who have lost the love of their life and survived the grief even when they thought they would die themself. They are women who have had to choose to stop the suffering of their baby and instead take on a lifetime of suffering themself. They are women who have overcome homelessness, abuse, and addiction, and have changed the course of their lives and now help others conquer the same. These women have overcome loss, mental illness, eating disorders, addictions, divorce, and cancer. They are women who have survived despite the odds against them. They are Great Canadian Women.

SHE SERIES AND HER SPECIAL EDITION SISTER SERIES

A collection of real-life stories from courageous women around the globe who confidently share their life experiences. Whether they have overcome life traumas, found a way through seemingly impossible circumstances, or embarked on the often turbulent entrepreneurial path, they have all bravely risen above their pain and fears. They no longer hide behind their own or other people's judgment but forge ahead, speaking their truth, making waves, moving mountains, and blazing trails while being the leaders they were always meant to be.